WEIGHT TRAINING

By the same author
Basic Fitness
Basic Judo
Basic Karate
The Complete Body Builder
Judo and Self Defence
Self Defence in the Home

WEIGHT TRAINING

E. G. Bartlett

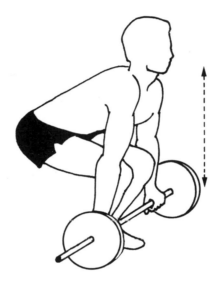

DAVID & CHARLES
Newton Abbot   London   North Pomfret (Vt)

British Library Cataloguing in Publication Data

Bartlett, E. G.
  Weight training.
  1. Weight lifting
  I. Title
  796.4'1   GV546.5

ISBN 0-7153-8512-7

© Text: E. G. Bartlett 1984

Typeset by Typesetters (Birmingham) Ltd
and printed in Great Britain
by Biddles Ltd, Guildford
for David & Charles (Publishers) Limited
Brunel House   Newton Abbot   Devon

Published in the United States of America
by David & Charles Inc
North Pomfret   Vermont 05053   USA

Contents

Introduction

People often confuse weight training with weight lifting but there is a difference. Weight training is using weights to promote muscular development, or to build up strength. Weight lifting is a competitive sport in which contestants strive to lift the heaviest weights in recognised competition lifts. Weight lifters certainly use weight training to prepare for their contests, indeed it is the only way to train for this sport, but others practise it for quite different purposes.

The most usual motive for taking up weight training is to keep fit or to build up one's body. For the latter purpose it is a sure way to success. Gains in physique sought by other methods usually take longer to bring about and are sometimes not as lasting. You would have to do a lot more 'free-standing' exercises, that is, exercises without the use of apparatus, to achieve the same results as if you used weights progressively. The only way to increase your work load by free-standing exercises is to increase the number of repetitions, whereas with weight training you can increase the work load by adding to the weight you are using.

Weight training can also help to correct faults in muscular development. For instance, if you have strong legs and weak arms, you can build up the latter. It can be used to develop stamina; circuit training as described in Chapter 11 is the usual way of doing this. And, increasingly, it is being used as an aid to other sports. Thirty years ago, athletes were a bit suspicious about weight training. It was believed that the use of

weights could lead to loss of agility and slower performances, the condition known as 'muscle-bound'. Very few top athletes ignore weight training today, however, as it has been found beneficial whatever their sport.

If you have any physical ailment at all or suspect any defect in your body, consult your doctor before embarking on any weight training course, and abide by his decision.

In this book we shall look at the equipment needed, the methods of training for various purposes, the basic principles of training, the muscles to be developed, the use of weights by women, general rules of diet and health, and at the sports of weight lifting and power lifting. First, however, let us consider the advantages of weights over other methods of training and learn the basic terminology of the subject.

As already mentioned, gains in physique made with weights are quicker and surer, and it has been said that such gains last a lifetime. There is also a greater variety of exercises to add to the interest of training. You can vary your schedule from time to time by substituting exercises from the same group. There are certainly fewer repetitions to be done, so your training period can be shortened because when the exercise you are doing becomes too easy, you simply make it difficult again by adding extra weight. You can devise progressive schedules easily, which is what you need for body building, since weights are usually available in units as small as 5lb or even 2lb. Weights will never weaken. Springs such as are used in chest expanders do weaken and of course they are weakening at the time when you are getting stronger, and even on the most expensive models there is a limit to the number or power of the strands that can be added to correct this. Weights never wear out as do metal or rubber strands. They last a lifetime and you can always add to your stock as need and finances allow. The only disadvantage of weights is that they are not easily portable and they take up a certain amount of room, which makes them unsuitable as a method of training for those who have to travel a lot, or who live in restricted accommodation such as, say, a bedsitter or high-rise flat. Such people could however carry out their training at a club. Most large towns boast such facilities.

Glossary

There are various terms used in weight training with which it is necessary to become familiar before reading further on the subject. Those most frequently met with are:

Bar The long rod, usually 5 or 6ft in length, on which the weights are loaded.
Barbell The bar when loaded with weights.
Collar The disc which screws onto the bar or dumb-bell rod to hold the weights in place.
Discs These are the round weights with a hole in the middle which fit onto the bar, and they are in various weights and sizes.
Dumb-bell rod A short bar, usually about a foot in length, which is loaded with weights secured by a collar each side of them, like the bar.
Dumb-bell The above rod when loaded.
Repetition The performance of an exercise once only.

Set A number of repetitions of one exercise.
Number of sets The number of times each set of repetitions is to be performed.
Point of resistance A term used in body building, where you do an exercise until you just cannot do another repetition. It is in fact this last one, that you just cannot manage, which develops your muscle.

The last four terms are used in describing how often the particular exercise is to be done. It is usual to write the information thus: 3×10. This means that you do ten repetitions of the exercise, rest a minute, do ten more, rest a minute, and then do ten more. There could of course be four sets of ten, or three sets to the 'point of resistance'.

There are other pieces of apparatus, the names of which we shall learn as we meet them, but the above are basic.

1 Equipment

If you decide to take up weight training, you can either join a club, which will have all the equipment you need, or train at home either alone or with a few friends. Your equipment can be as basic or as comprehensive as you like to make it, and when we come to the exercises in this book, you will find that variations are indicated according to what you have to work with.

Essential Equipment

The essentials are: a bar; dumb-bell rods; eight collars so that you can lock weights onto two dumb-bells, four collars being needed for each dumb-bell rod, two inside the weights and two outside; a variety of weights, totalling at least 120lb to begin with; and a bench, which can be an ordinary flat bench, long enough to lie on with your feet on the floor at one end and wide enough to support you.

With these basics you can make a beginning and, if you wish, do all the training you will ever need, apart from possibly adding to your stock of weights as your strength increases (which would be necessary only in the case of a body builder who needed the increased resistances to work against, or a weight lifter who would have to use heavier and heavier weights). The cost of even these basic essentials today might well be in the region of £100, but you can sometimes pick up equipment cheaply if you study the small ads in the body building magazines, or in *Exchange and Mart*, or you could even advertise your needs in your local paper. Second-hand weight sets are just as good for your purpose as

new ones, but make sure that the collars have not rusted. There are two types of collar, one of which fastens by screwing down a peg, and the other by use of an Alan key. Make sure they work and that they hold firm. New ones can of course be bought separately.

One of the points to look for in buying equipment is that you get standard sized rods and weights. Some firms have made their rods slightly too small or too large, so that only their discs and collars will fit. This is to force you to buy all your extras from them, of course, but you will be in difficulty if they go out of business, since discs obtained elsewhere will not then fit your rods.

Having just one bar and two dumb-bell rods means that you have to be prepared to change your weights on the bar from exercise to exercise. It helps therefore to increase your number of bars and discs when you can afford to, and to have various bars made up with different weights. You will use a much heavier load in exercises like the squat or the dead lift than you will need for the curl or the triceps curl. Your various bars are best stored in a rack. You may find squat stands useful. These are metal or wooden uprights with a groove in the top in which you rest the weight. You simply walk between the uprights to either take the weight, or lay it down. These are extremely useful if you are working alone as they will enable you to handle the heavier weights.

As long as you are prepared to put up with the extra work of changing discs, money is better spent first on the following items of equipment:

Iron boots These are iron platforms with straps to attach them to the soles of your own boots or shoes and provide extra weight on your legs to make the muscles work harder. The more advanced models have a hole through the plate horizontally from side to side, through which you can fit a dumb-bell rod and attach heavier weights on either side.

Inclined bench This is a bench which may be adjusted to various angles and which you can lie back against when exercising. A fixed board could be set up to serve the same purpose.

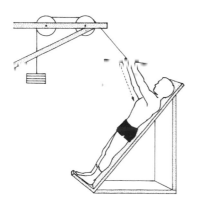

Neck harness Weights are suspended from canvas straps which are fitted over the top of the head and around the forehead.

Wrist roller A short rod, to the centre of which is attached a cord on which you can hang weights.

The following equipment is rather more sophisticated and extremely valuable for training purposes if available:

Leg-pressing machine This apparatus consists of a platform which moves up and down between uprights. It can be pegged at a suitable height and loaded with weights. By lying on your back

11

under it, bending your knees, and placing your feet against the underside of the platform, you can push it up and down. The pegs prevent the platform from falling down far enough to damage the legs.

Pulley and weights There are two pulleys in the ceiling over which there passes a stout wire which is attached at one end to weights and at the other to a bar which you can grasp with both hands.

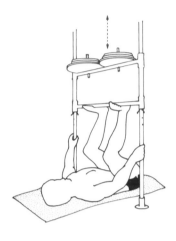

Calf machine This consists of a pair of shafts joined together and hinged at the wall. On these you suspend suitable weights and then rest the ends of the shafts on your shoulders so you are taking the weight.

If you are taking up weight training to develop your physique, a weighing machine or bathroom scales and a tape measure would help you to assess progress, but these are already found in most homes. A large full-length mirror in which you can watch your performance, and which helps you to concentrate on the muscles being used, is also an essential in body building.

There is a great advantage in having a training partner, since with someone to take the weight off you, you can use much heavier poundages in such exercises as the bench press and the squat. It is worth considering whether you know anyone who might like to train with you. If not, someone might be found by advertising. You would need a place to train, of course, but it could be a room in your house, a garage or a loft. Between you, it might be possible to buy a more comprehensive range of equipment. Certainly the encouragement you would receive from having a training

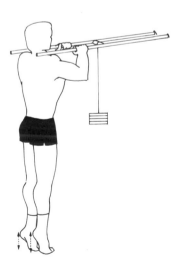

partner would help you to go on, in those moments when you might feel that not enough progress was being made.

If there is a group of you and there is no existing club in your neighbourhood, you might like to consider forming one. Your association can just be the loose one of a group of friends who train together, but if there are more than four or five, some form of organisation will be needed. You will want to know who owns the equipment, who is responsible for rent, heating and so on, and how new members are to be elected or undesirable ones excluded. Without some basic rules like this, you could meet difficulty in the future.

You will need warm, airy premises where you can leave your equipment safely and the kind of structure where you can rig up your pulley and calf machine. Non-slip floor covering is essential. Rooms can be hired from the YMCA, though they sometimes prefer to take over the club and run it as one of their activities. Church halls can sometimes be hired reasonably. Lofts and cellars can be converted into quite acceptable gymnasia, with a little effort.

If you are forming a club like this,

have as many bars and dumb-bell rods as possible, each made up with a different poundage, and store them in a rack, labelled with the poundage. Start with as low as 20lb and go up in 5lb stages to 200lb or more. Make sure members replace them after use.

Have at least one leg-pressing machine, one calf machine, one neck harness, one wrist roller, one bench and one incline bench, and set up a pulley, with the facility for attaching varying weights. With a little organisation, one member can be using one piece of apparatus while somebody else uses another; the only pieces you need plenty of are the bars and weights. Mirrors on the wall and a notice board are added refinements. A pair of bathroom scales will enable you to record progress in the club itself.

If body building is the main preoccupation of your members, it is encouraging to keep records of progress. Take a member's measurements and weight when he joins, and record progress month by month. A study of these records in years to come will teach you more about body building than any textbook.

2 Basic Principles

Before starting weight training, it is well to have a general idea of how it works. The human body grows naturally from infancy to the age of twenty-one or twenty-two and its development in this time is influenced partly by hereditary and partly by environmental factors. This development will naturally be helped by good food, fresh air, adequate rest and exercise. When normal growth stops, if we want to develop further, we have to undertake planned exercise.

When we exercise a muscle, tissue within that muscle is broken down. Nature is a wonderful healer, however, and as that tissue is built up again, from the food and oxygen we take in, just a little bit more is built up than we have broken down. If we then break it down again with more exercise, nature again builds a little more, and so it goes on, causing the muscle to grow. That, very simply, is the process behind body building.

It is dependent on the right kind of exercise, on adequate rest to allow nature to rebuild and on the proper intake of food and oxygen. We must look after our general health; digestive and excretory systems must be in order; if teeth are decayed, they must be seen to at once, or every mouthful eaten will carry poisons into the system. This may sound a trivial thing, but bad teeth can undo all the work of a body builder.

We should consider at this point what we want from weight training. Do we simply want to keep fit? Any exercise will help us in that and the simple routine given in Chapter 9 will be sufficient, varying the exercises from time to time to maintain interest. Do we want to develop stamina? Circuit training (see Chapter 11) is the method for this. Do we want to make weight training an aid to some other sport? The suggestions in Chapters 12 and 13 will help. Do we want to build up physique or to correct weaknesses in development? Chapter 10 outlines the way, but there is a little more to be understood in this case, before a start is made.

Years ago, strong men toured the music halls, giving exhibitions which fired young men to emulate them. These young men took courses, but often they got nowhere because in those days courses consisted of what would now be called 'one-set systems'. There was an exercise for the arms, one for the legs, one for the chest and so on, and all men whatever their size did the same set of exercises, the only difference being that big men used heavier weights. It so happened that this method suited the big men and they grew bigger, but the small man, however enthusiastically he tried, got nowhere.

Modern training is more scientific. It is recognised that men of different bone structure need differently planned courses. You must first decide what type you are. If you are the big-boned, fat man, then you will be what is called an endomorph. If you are the thin, small-boned, nervous type, then you will be an ectomorph. If you are in between, you are a mesomorph, the athletic type of person.

You must do the exercises specified for your particular type, if you wish to succeed. It means in general that the big fat man will be called upon to do a lot of repetitions with a light weight. This will not come easily to him. He would prefer to do less repetitions with a heavy weight. The thin man on the other hand will have to do few repetitions with a heavy weight, and being an energetic nervous type, he would prefer to do a lot more with a weight he could handle more easily. It is essential however to stick strictly to type training, if you want to build up physique or improve your body.

When Should You Train?
This will largely depend on individual circumstances. If you are doing the simple keep fit course in Chapter 9, early in the morning, on arising, would be satisfactory. If you are doing serious body building, or circuit training, or training to assist another sport, then your schedule will take longer, and the evening would be more satisfactory. Try to allow an hour and a half after your meal, however, and give yourself a period of relaxation between finishing your training and going to bed.

How Often
It depends on your purpose. The simple keep fit scheme can be followed every day, body building or circuit training every other day. Training to assist other sports should be no more than twice a week and should not be on the same nights as other training. The every other day routine is absolutely essential for body builders. If you try to do it every day, you will defeat your purpose, because this will not give your body time to rebuild.

Where Should You Train?
The ideal is of course a gymnasium where you have other training partners and all the equipment to hand. If you are training alone or with just a few friends, however, try to do so in a quiet room, warm enough for comfort, but with plenty of fresh air. Try to avoid a room heated by gas or oil burners, as these will eat up the oxygen you need. Do have the windows open. Your body desperately needs air when you are doing heavy training. Train in front of a mirror if you are body building. There are two reasons for this. First, you can see if you are doing the exercise correctly; secondly, it helps to watch the muscle working and to concentrate your attention on its development.

What Should You Wear?
Loose clothes are the answer, and as few as possible. If it is warm enough, loose shorts or bathing trunks are satisfactory. If it is cooler, a track suit is ideal. Remember that your body wants to breathe, not only through your nose, but also through your pores. If you are wrapped up in too many clothes, the air cannot reach you. Put on something warm in between exercises or when resting. Train in boots or shoes with a heel, particularly if handling heavy weights, or you will run the risk of becoming flat-footed.

What Weights Should You Use?
There is a simple way of working this out. With each exercise try loading the bar or the dumb-bell rod with weights until you reach a point where you can just perform the exercise once with an effort, and once only. Note the weight, and the weight you should be using can be calculated from that as follows: if you are a small, thin-boned man (the ectomorph) use between 60 per cent and 70 per cent of this maximum; if you are the medium type (the mesomorph) take off 5lb; if you are the big fellow (the endomorph) take off 10lb.

How Long Does It Take to See Progress?
This depends on type; big men develop quickest, the medium type next, and little men are slowest. But do not be impatient and do not try to hurry nature's progress. You certainly cannot hasten things by training twice as often; you will only undo the good you are

doing. If you keep records of your measurements, six months should show really encouraging gains; two years should see you approaching your peak, at three nights training per week.

What Measurements Should You Take?
The following give a guide to development: height, weight, neck, around the chest across the nipples, waist, hips, upper arm straight, upper arm bent, forearm, wrist, thigh, calf and ankle. Take measurements before training, not after, and if possible get someone else to do it for you. The chest should be measured normally at first and then expanded by breathing in. The difference is more important than the basic, in terms of health.

What Proportions Can You Hope to Achieve?
This is a question that all body builders ask. If they are going to devote three nights a week to training for two years, they want to know what they can expect. The answer depends first of all on the basic type of physique, secondly on perseverance at training, and thirdly on age. The younger you are, the better your chances, though it is inadvisable to start using heavy weights before the age of eighteen, and once you have passed the age of twenty-six, your bone structure is fixed; you can then build only on the muscles you have. Quite pleasing results can still be obtained, however.

Below are some guidelines to the measurements which could be aimed for. These suggestions are only a rough guide. If you can do better, then well and good. You may find, too, that you do not exactly fit into a category. You might be an ectomorph verging on a mesomorph, and then, although thin and weak to begin with, you might make sensational gains.

Mental Approach to Training
Success in anything depends a lot on mental attitude. Certainly this is true of weight training. Patience, perseverance and real enthusiasm are needed. This is where having a partner would encourage you. An enthusiasm shared tends to live, but if you are training alone you can still succeed if you bring to the task three things: determination, hope and concentration.

Make up your mind that you are going to train. Set aside the time needed for this and let nothing interfere. It will need resolution and self-discipline to begin with but training will soon become a habit and, as the results begin to show, your determination to carry on will grow. Avoid the temptation to put off training one night for a trivial reason, such as wanting to see something on television or feeling too tired. It is no use saying you will do twice as much the next night to make up for it, because even if you did this, you would only over-exhaust yourself.

	Small *ectomorph*	Medium *mesomorph*	Large *endomorph*
height	5ft 7in	5ft 10in	6ft
weight	140lb	170lb	190lb
neck	14½in	16½in	17in
chest, normal	38in	42in	46in
chest, expanded	40in	45in	49in
waist	28in	31in	34in
hips	32in	36in	38in
upper arm, straight	11½in	13in	14½in
upper arm, flexed	13½in	15in	16in
forearm	11in	12in	13½in
wrist	6½in	7in	7½in
thigh	19in	21in	24½in
calf	13½in	14½in	16in
ankle	8in	8½in	9½in

Whether you are training for body building or to improve some sport, keep your ambition before you and understand that success is certain. Weight training is a game where there are no losers because as soon as you pick up a weight and do an exercise you are making that tiny bit of progress.

If you are body building and, after a couple of months, you can see only tiny improvements on your tape measure (or even a decrease in some measurements, because initially the training may get rid of excess fat) it is easy to feel that such small results are not worth the effort. Do not give way to this kind of despair. Although the process may sometimes seem discouragingly slow, it is taking place.

When you are actually training, concentrate. Put aside all distracting thoughts and worries. Do not allow anyone to chatter to you or to interrupt you. Train in a quiet room away from the television or radio. If you are building your body, look at the muscles you are using in your mirror.

If you are training with partners, resist the temptation to compete. Use the weight and the number of repetitions that are appropriate to your course and let others do the same. In that way you will avoid any risk of strain.

Cultivate a spirit of calmness in your daily living. The result of worry and rush can be ulcers. Try to keep a sense of proportion. Most of the trivial annoyances that spoil a day are not worth a second thought.

You will realise by now that the self-discipline and effort demanded by weight training are going to have effects on your character beyond the mere physical gains to your body.

Diet

We are what we eat. The truth is as simple as that. If we are underweight or underdeveloped, we need to eat more as well as to weight train in order to build up; if we are overweight, we need to eat less, as well as to exercise.

The body needs proteins to build and replace tissue, so a weight trainer's diet must be rich in these; starches and sugar are needed for energy; fats will build up reserves and keep us warm; vitamins keep us healthy; and we need small quantities of minerals, water and roughage. It is largely a matter of taste how we take these essential requirements. Our bodies will soon tell us if we are doing wrong; hunger and thirst are felt and satisfied before any harm is done, but illness comes on more slowly and the only way to guard against it is to have an elementary idea of your daily needs, and to see that you satisfy them.

Proteins are chemical compounds of carbon, oxygen, hydrogen and nitrogen, combined with other elements such as phosphorus and sulphur. Protein molecules are built up of amino acids, which are broken down in the stomach and intestines and then combined again in different formulae to create the various kinds of protein needed to build up different cells in our bodies. Thus some will become muscle cells, some blood cells and so on.

The daily protein requirement of an active young man, such as a weight trainer might be, is 90g; for a woman it is 12g less. To talk of so many grams of protein, however, does not mean very much, because it is only part of any food source and much of the rest is water. Meat contains about 7g of protein per ounce, so an 8oz steak would give you 56g. Cheese has the same value as meat; an egg contains 7g. There are many books giving tables of values, so it is pointless to detail them all here.

Carbohydrates with fats give us energy. The unit of measurement given in diets is the calorie. There are three groups of carbohydrates: monosaccharides, disaccharides and polysaccharides, but since they can only be absorbed in their simplest forms as monosaccharides, the more complex forms are broken down. The quantities we need have to be considered in conjunction with fats. About 50 per cent of our energy is provided by carbohydrate intake, 35 to 40 per cent by fats, and the rest from protein foods. A moderately active man needs 3,000 calories per day, a very active one 3,600 calories; a normally active woman needs 2,200 calories, a very active one 2,500.

Our main mineral needs are calcium to build and repair bones and teeth and to help the blood clot if injury occurs; iron for the red corpuscles of the blood; and phosphorus which is used in the chemical reactions that turn food into energy. Apart from these, we need many others, in minute quantities, such as cobalt, copper, zinc, manganese, iodine, fluorine and salts. Our daily needs of calcium and iron are large enough to be measured. Men and women need the same: 600mg of calcium per day (except that a woman needs more when pregnant) and 15mg of iron.

Vitamins are required in very small quantities and their absence leads to deficiency diseases. There are about twenty-seven identified vitamins, of which seven are known to be essential and the rest presumed to be so. Vitamin A keeps the skin and breathing passages healthy; vitamin B is a complex group combating various diseases; vitamin C builds healthy tissue; vitamin D aids the digestion of calcium; vitamin E is believed to be necessary for the reproductive system; vitamin K makes the blood clot; and vitamin P is needed to make the capillaries strong.

Water is needed for all cell functions and the chemical processes of the body. Our bodies are composed of between 55 and 70 per cent water, and whilst we could live for some weeks without food, we could not live for more than a few days without water. We require an intake of at least 4 pints a day.

Roughage is the name given to indigestible fibres. They simply pass through the body but in so doing they help to eliminate waste and keep us from becoming constipated.

Where do we get these daily require-ments? Proteins are found mainly in dairy products such as cheese, milk and eggs; in vegetables, particularly peanuts, beans, peas, carrots, cabbages and soya beans; and in meat and fish. Starches and sugar come from bread, potatoes, honey, preserves and so on. Fats come from butter, fat meat, milk and lard. Vitamins come from vegetables and fruits, fish oils, lean meat, and again from dairy products. Minerals are found in all the above foods and in water. There is enough roughage in a well-rounded diet but more can be added in the form of bran if it is felt necessary. Water is present in all foods and drinks, but the weight trainer should consider the advantage of drinking pure water and avoiding tea or coffee which are stimulants.

How are we to work out what the above quantities are in terms of everyday meals? The following will be a rough guide. An average woman needs each day: ½ pint of milk, 1oz of cheese, 1 egg, 4oz of meat or fish, 4oz of green vegetables or citrus fruit, 4oz of bread, 4oz of potatoes, 2oz of butter or margarine. An average man needs the same, but with 6oz each of bread and potatoes and 3oz of butter or margarine.

There are many books on diet and many arguments in favour of vegetarian diets, vegan diets, food reform and so on. It would be out of place to enter into these arguments here. Athletes have thrived with and without meat, and it is largely a matter of choice. We do need, however, to consider how many additives there are in modern processed food, such as colouring matter, preservatives and chemical flavourings. The nearer we can get to natural organically grown food, the more healthy we are likely to be, since pesticides used on farms find their way in minute traces into the produce. If you are not making the progress you expect in weight training, it is worth looking into any dietary changes you could make and reading more on the subject.

A few points only will be given here:

(a) Brown wholemeal bread is better than white, if possible made with natural stone-ground flour.

(b) Cooking lessens the nutritional value of food. Steaming is the best method, since it preserves most of the natural goodness; fried food should be eaten only in moderation.

(c) Raw vegetable salads are of great value. Even vegetables such as cabbages, onions or swedes, which are normally cooked, are quite tasty in salads.

(d) Plain foods are better than highly flavoured or spiced ones.

(e) An occasional day's fast is beneficial.

(f) Eating slowly is recommended.

General Health

The rules for achieving and maintaining good health are simple but it is still worth remembering how important it is to observe them. Plenty of fresh air, exercise and rest are absolutely vital. Try to spend time in the countryside or by the sea and practise taking deep breaths of fresh air. It is helpful to expose the whole body to the air at least once a day. We breathe through all the pores in the skin as well as through the nose. Air tones up the skin and induces a feeling of relaxation and well-being. Sleep with the window open and try to get a good night's sleep. Avoid over-indulgence in bad habits such as drinking and smoking, and strike a balance between mental and physical activities. The ancient Greeks had a threefold view of man which incorporated body, mind and spirit. It was thought necessary to develop each of these spheres to its limit in order to achieve a well-balanced life of health and happiness.

3 Muscles of the Body

There are three kinds of muscles in the body: voluntary, involuntary and cardiac. The involuntary and the cardiac ones are found internally and carry on such functions as making us breathe, digest and excrete food, and pumping blood around the veins, even while we are asleep. Without their unceasing labours we should not be alive, but apart from paying attention to general health, there is not much we can do about them. It is the voluntary muscles that concern the weight trainer, because these are the ones he hopes to develop.

What is a muscle? It is made up of what is commonly called 'flesh'. The meat we eat is the muscle and the fat of animals. Its composition is hundreds of minute cells arranged in fibres and surrounded by a protective sheath. Bundles of these fibres are covered with a connecting tissue and they are bound together in another tissue. Muscles are attached to the bones by tendons at either end. Each muscle has an origin and an insertion. When a muscle contracts it shortens and so pulls closer together the two bones to which it is attached. As one bone usually offers more resistance than the other, the one with the least resistance moves. The muscle is then said to have its origin on the bone that stays still and its insertion on the bone that moves.

A simple example of the above is seen if we bend an arm. The bicep, which is the muscle at the front between the shoulder and the elbow, contracts and, the shoulder remaining still, the elbow is bent. The biceps would be said to have their origin at the shoulder bone and their insertion at the elbow.

But muscles do not work in isolation. Usually a whole group are involved. The muscle at the back of the upper arm is the triceps. When we bend our arm as described above, this tends to keep the motion under control, so that it is not a violent movement. In this respect it acts in opposition to the biceps.

Before setting about weight training, it will help if you learn to identify each of your muscles and consider the job each one does. Strip off and stand in front of a mirror. If you are inclined to be fat or are not very well developed, you may not be able to pick out all your muscles, but identify as many as you can, and learn where the others are (*see* Diagrams A and B).

Sterno mastoids These are seen in the neck. They enable the head to be turned from side to side or lifted up and down.
Trapezius This muscle covers the shoulder and the upper part of the back of the neck. It helps in the head turning movement and also in any arm movement.
Deltoids These bands of muscle cover the shoulder joints. They enable you to raise your arm sideways or, holding it straight, to raise it in front of you to shoulder level.
Biceps Bend your arm. The muscle that you see bulging out in the upper arm is the bicep. That is its function, to enable you to bend your arm at the elbow joint.
Triceps The muscle at the back of the upper arm which enables you to straighten the arm at the elbow joint after you have bent it. You may be able

to make it stand out sufficiently to see, if you hold your arm straight and press back on the wrist.

Pectorals The big triangular muscles at the front of the chest. They can be more readily seen on the male if you place your hands on your hips and drop your shoulders slightly forward. They enable you to move your arms forwards and to pull your arms into your body.

Serratus magnus These little ridges of muscle can be seen on the sides of the body under the armpits. They help you to lift your arms sideways.

Supinator longus The muscle at the side and back of the forearm. It enables you to turn your wrist from side to side.

Flexors of the forearm These are found at the front of the forearm. They enable you to bend your wrist inwards; if you cannot see them, you can feel them by gently placing the fingers of the other hand on the inside of your forearm as you bend your wrist inwards.

External oblique abdominals Extending from the lower ribs down the side of the body, these enable you to turn your body from side to side, or to bend sideways and to straighten up again.

Upper and lower abdominals At the front of the body, extending from the lower ribs to the pubic bone, these muscles enable you to bend forwards, to sit up if you are lying flat, or to raise your legs out in front of you.

Pectineus and adductor longus The muscles on the inside of the upper thigh which move the thigh inwards.

Rectus femoris The long muscle running down the front of the thigh. It is used in movements from the hip joint, such as raising the leg forwards, or straightening the leg out in front of you, when the knee is raised.

Vastus internus Found at the side and back of the upper leg, it enables you to turn your leg.

Peroneus longus The muscle at the side of the lower leg. Together with other muscles in this area, it enables you to move the foot and to rotate the leg.

Tibialis anticus The big muscle at the

front of the calf which helps you to bend the foot upwards.

Gastrocnemius and soleus These are at the side and back of the calf. The gastrocnemius flexes the foot, so that you can bend it backwards, and the main function of the soleus is to enable you to retain an upright posture.

Infra spinatus and rhomboideus major Muscles at the back of the shoulder (Diagram B), which enable you to take your shoulders back and assist with any pulling action.

Latissimus dorsi The large muscles at the back of the body which enable you to rotate your body and to raise the arms. If you are underdeveloped, building up your latissimus dorsi, or 'lats' as body builders call them, will give you a broader chest.

Erector spinae The muscle group in the small of the back. These enable you to straighten up after bending forwards.

Gluteus medius and gluteus maximus The fleshy muscles of the buttocks. They help you to rotate and move the legs.

Vastus lateralis Found at the side and back of the upper leg, it assists in bending the knee and enables you to raise the leg sideways from the hip joint.

Adductor magnus The muscle at the back of the inside of the upper leg. It enables you to turn the leg, as in pointing the foot outwards.

Biceps of the leg and the semi-tendinosus These two muscles are at the back of the upper leg. They fulfil a similar function in the leg to the biceps in the arm, enabling you to bend your leg backwards at the knee joint.

Tensor muscles and vastus externus The tensor is the muscle over the hip, and the vastus externus runs from it down the outside of the thigh. They enable you to lift the leg sideways.

The above are of course only the main muscles. There are over two hundred pairs. Many of these others combine with the ones mentioned in helping you to perform any movement. It often

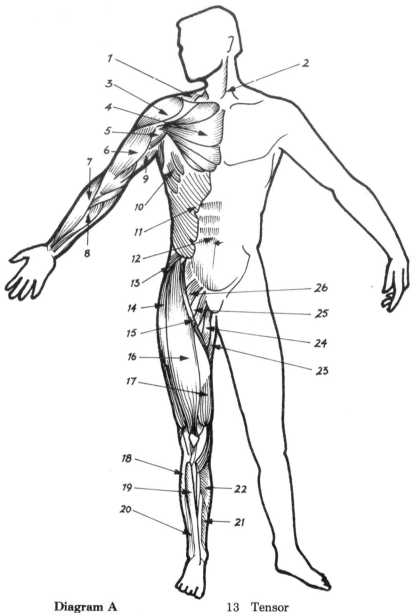

Diagram A
Anterior aspect

1	Trapezius	13	Tensor
2	Sterno cleido mastoid	14	Vastus externus
3	Deltoid	15	Sartorius
4	Pectoralis major	16	Rectus femoris
5	Coraco brachialis	17	Vastus internus
6	Biceps	18	Peroneus longus
7	Supinator longus	19	Tibialis anticus
8	Flexors	20	Peroneus brevis
9	Triceps	21	Soleus
10	Serratus magnus	22	Gastrocnemius
11	External oblique	23	Adductor magnus
12	Rectus abdominus	24	Gracillis
		25	Adductor longus
		26	Pectineus

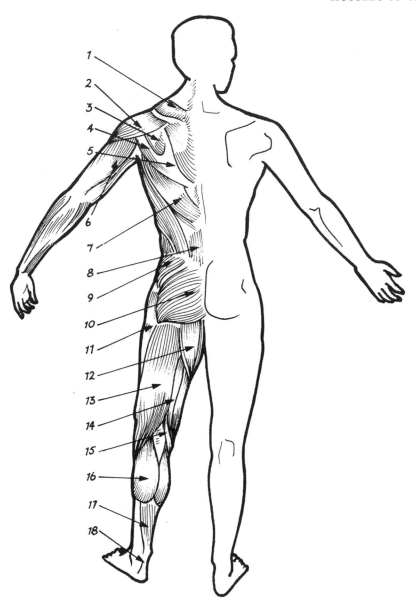

Diagram B
Posterior aspect

1	Trapezius	9	Gluteus medius
2	Deltoid	10	Gluteus maximus
3	Infra spinatus	11	Vastus lateralis
4	Teres major	12	Adductor magnus
5	Rhomboideus major	13	Biceps
6	Triceps	14	Semi-tendinosus
7	Latissimus dorsi	15	Semi-membranosus
8	Erector spinae	16	Gastrocnemius
		17	Soleus
		18	Tendo achillus

happens that while some of the muscles in your body are performing the movement, others are holding the rest of your body still.

The ability to recognise these muscles will help the weight trainer in three ways. First, he can perform the exercise correctly, since he knows which muscle he is using and for what purpose. Secondly, he can concentrate his attention on this particular muscle and this in itself assists development. (The reason manual workers are not always big men is because they are concentrating on their work and not on the muscles they are using at any moment.) Thirdly, the weight trainer can see which of his muscles especially need developing and can concentrate on them. If, for example, you are conscious of being thin and small chested, you will know that you need to develop your pectorals and your latissimus dorsi, and that doing so will vastly improve your appearance.

Of course, you should not rush into giving concentrated attention to one particular muscle group without first doing a general course of training. Read on to Chapters 8 to 14 before planning any course.

4 Exercises for the Chest and Shoulders

This and the following three chapters will explain exercises for various muscle groups. It must be appreciated, however, that any exercise may benefit muscles in other groups as well, and that the grouping in this book is on the basis of the principal use of the exercise.

Do not attempt to do all the exercises in any one of these chapters all at once. Refer to Chapters 9 to 14 to learn how you should select and combine the exercises for various purposes. Read also the information in Chapter 2 on how and when to train.

This will enable you to get the maximum benefit from training sessions and avoid risking any injuries. Load the bar with the appropriate weight as directed there (see page 15).

Exercise 1 Bent Over Rowing
Stand upright, feet normal distance apart. Pick up the bar, hands shoulder width apart, palms on top of the bar, fingers over, thumbs underneath. Bend forwards until the body is at right angles to the legs and parallel to the ground. Keep the back flat and stay in this forward position with the arms holding the bar hanging down. Now bring the bar up to your chest by bending your elbows, breathing out as you do so. Lower to the hanging position, breathing in. Do not put the bar on the ground between repetitions.

This exercise particularly benefits the latissimus dorsi, the trapezius and the triceps, and is good for the chest because of the deep breathing involved.

Fig 1

Exercise 2 Upright Rowing

Stand upright, feet close together. Grip the bar with both hands close together near the centre. Make sure that it balances as you lift it. Have your fingers over the bar and thumbs underneath as in **Exercise 1**. Let the bar hang in front of your thighs. Take a deep breath and, as you breathe out, bring the bar up level with your shoulders, raising the elbows outwards. Try to make the bar touch your chin and keep it as near to the body as possible. Breathe in as you lower to the hanging position. Do not replace the bar on the ground between repetitions. This exercise particularly benefits the deltoids and pectorals.

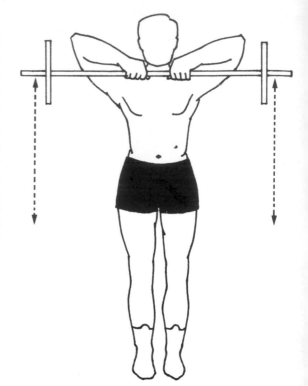

Fig 2

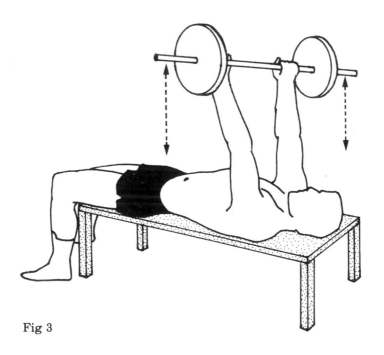

Fig 3

Exercise 3 Bench Press

Lie on a bench, with the upper body and shoulders firmly supported by it, and the feet on the floor off the end. Take a wide grip on the bar, with fingers over and thumbs underneath, and have it on the chest fairly high up, not down towards the abdomen. With the bar on the chest, take a deep breath and breathe out as you push it upwards to arm's length. Breathe in as you lower.

If you are body building and want to do this to the point of resistance, then you will see the advantage here of having partners to take the bar off you at the last movement which you just cannot manage. If working alone you will have to lower it to the chest and ease it down towards your stomach so that you can sit up. This is an excellent exercise for the whole of the chest area, particularly the pectorals, triceps and even some of the back muscles. It is a great favourite for all sports training.

Exercise 4 Crucifix with Dumb-bells

Lie on the bench as in **Exercise 3**, feet firmly on the floor. Take a dumb-bell in each hand and hold the arms out sideways level with the shoulders. Take a deep breath. As you breathe out, raise the dumb-bells to arm's length in front of your chest, keeping the arms straight. Breathe in again as you lower to the sides. Control the movement and do not let the weights pull the arms back suddenly to the floor. The arms should not drop back behind the shoulders. This is an excellent exercise for the pectorals.

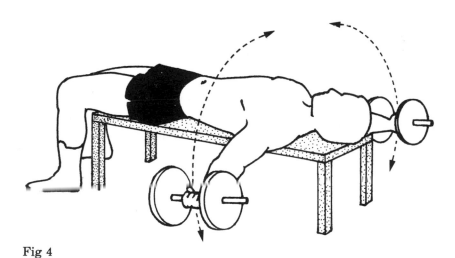

Fig 4

Exercise 5 Straight Arm Pullovers

Load your weights onto the centre of the dumb-bell rod and secure with a collar each side. Lie on the bench as for **Exercise 3.** Grip the dumb-bell rod at each end, palms facing your feet, so that the fingers curl over the top. Take it down your body to arm's length. Keeping the arms straight, take it up and over your head and behind your body, as far back as you can, breathing in as you do so. Then bring it forwards again, with arms straight, right down onto your lower body, breathing out. Make sure your hips do not leave the bench.

A good exercise for the pectorals, this also builds up all the shoulder muscles and the ribcage. It is useful therefore for those who want to develop their chest and, because of the deep breathing, it is invaluable for athletics and sports.

Exercise 6 Bent Arm Pullovers

Load the dumb-bell rod centrally, securing with a collar each side. Lie on the bench as for **Exercise 3** in such a position that your head is near the end of the bench. Grip the dumb-bell rod with as narrow a grip as possible, elbows bent, upper arms vertical, forearms at right angles with palms facing your head. Lower the dumb-bell over your head, bending your elbows. Breathe in as you do so. Then bring the weight back to the starting position over your chest, keeping the arms bent at the elbows. Breathe out as you do this.

This is what is called a short range movement, unlike the last exercise which was a full range movement. It is used for the triceps and for the chest in general.

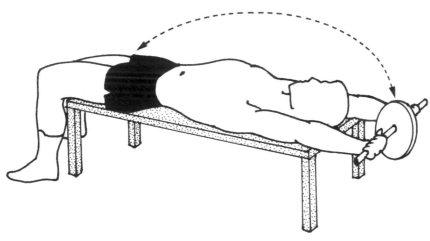

Fig 5

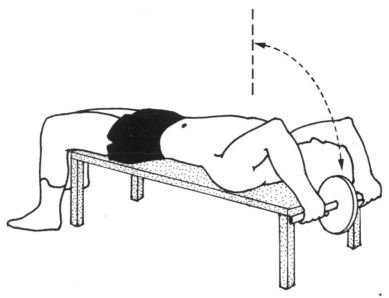

Fig 6

Exercise 7 Alternate Dumb-bell Presses
Stand with feet normally spaced. Take a
dumb-bell in each hand and bring them
up to rest on the shoulders. Press the
right hand as high as you can above the
head and as you bring it back to the
shoulder, press the left hand up above
the head. Breathe freely as you are doing
this exercise. Keep the body upright and
so that you do not lose balance keep the
dumb-bells as near the head as possible.

This works the upper back muscles,
the chest and the deltoids.

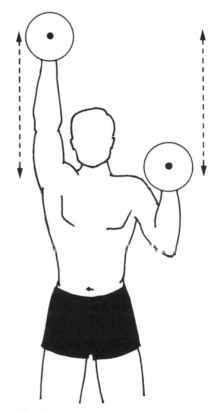

Fig 7

29

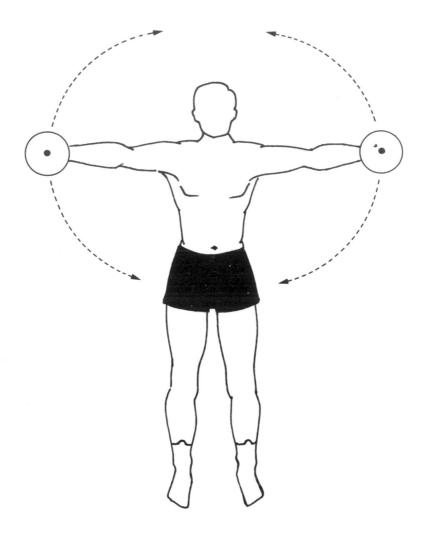

Fig 8

Exercise 8 Lateral Raises

Stand with the feet astride. Take a dumb-bell in each hand, letting them hang down at the sides, palms in towards your body. Raise them sideways until they are level with your waist, and at this point turn your wrists so that your palms are upwards, and carry on the movement raising the dumb-bells above the head, when the palms will be facing inwards towards each other. Breathe out as you raise and in as you lower again. Make the turn of the wrists at waist level both raising and lowering.

This is a full range movement for the latissimus dorsi and the deltoids in particular.

Exercise 9 Forward and Upward Swing with Dumb-bells

Stand upright, feet normal distance apart. Take a dumb-bell in each hand, palms facing the body, knuckles away from you. Raise each dumb-bell alternately, forwards and upwards to shoulder level and then on to above your head, in one continuous movement. As you lower one hand, raise the other. Breathe freely.

This is used for all the shoulder muscles and for the pectorals.

Exercise 10 Single Hand Rowing

Lean forwards at the waist and rest one hand on a bench, table, or the back of a chair. Take a dumb-bell in the other hand, palm towards your body, and let it hang down at arm's length. Bring it up to shoulder level, breathing out as you come up and in as you lower to arm's length again. Stay in a bent-over position, and after doing a set with one hand, change hands and do a set with the other.

This exercise is for the latissimus dorsi.

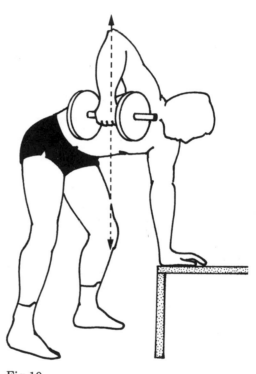

Fig 10

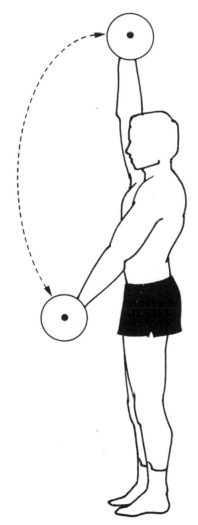

Fig 9

31

Exercise 11 Pull to Chest using Pulley and Weights

This exercise and the next two use a pulley and weights.

The pull to chest can be performed seated or even kneeling if you wish, as an alternative to standing, but Figure 11 illustrates the exercise standing as that is the basic position. Take a wide grip on the bar, knuckles uppermost. Start with arms out in front of you. Breathe in as you pull the bar to touch your chest, against the resistance of the weights. Breathe out as you straighten your arms again.

As well as working the deltoids and latissimus dorsi, this is also a deep breathing exercise, of course, so benefits the chest.

Exercise 12 Pull to Back of Neck using Pulley and Weights

Either kneel or sit for this exercise. Take a wide grip on the bar, knuckles uppermost. Start with arms at full length in front of you and pull the bar towards you, taking it over your head to the back of your neck. Breathe in as you pull and out as you straighten your arms again.

This uses the latissimus dorsi, shoulders and arms.

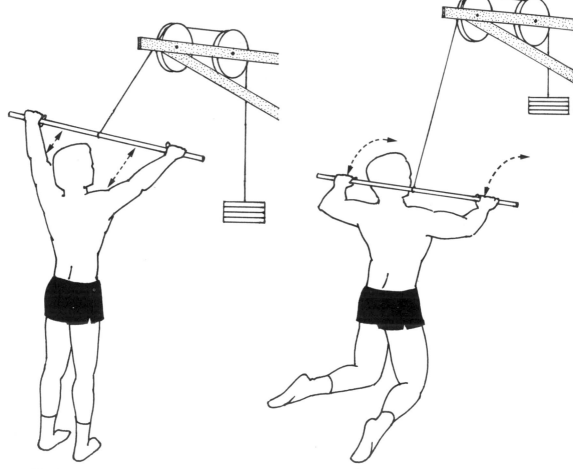

Fig 11   Fig 12

Exercise 13 Pull to Chest on Incline Bench

This uses not only the pulley and weights but also an incline bench.

Take a shoulder width grip on the bar, knuckles downwards. Breathe in as you pull it to your chest and out as you straighten your arms.

Again you will work the deltoids and latissimus dorsi, and your breathing will benefit. Note that if you take a narrow grip in this exercise, it can also be used for the biceps, as it then becomes equivalent to curling (see page 35).

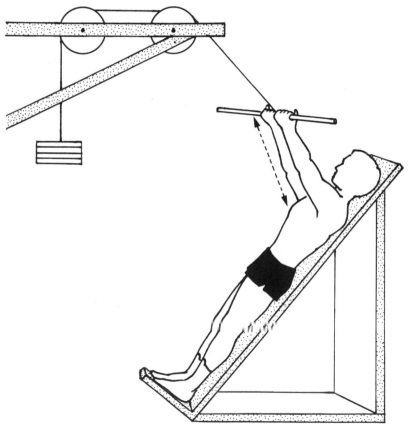

Fig 13

5 Exercises for the Arms and Wrists

Although the following exercises will principally benefit the arms and wrists they will use other muscles as well. Do not attempt to do them all at the same time, but refer to Chapters 9 to 14 for information on how to select the exercises you need.

Exercise 14 Clean with Barbell
Stand with the feet normal distance apart and underneath the bar, toes pointing to the front. Grip the bar with both hands shoulder width apart, bending the knees to do so. The knuckles are uppermost and the thumbs under the bar. Straighten the knees and lift the bar to a position high across the shoulders, in line with the Adam's apple. As the bar passes your waist level twist your wrists, so that the weight of it is

mostly on the balls of your thumbs. This movement is done quickly. When the bar is in position across your shoulders this is called 'the clean'.

As well as helping the arms and wrists, this exercise also helps the back and the leg muscles.

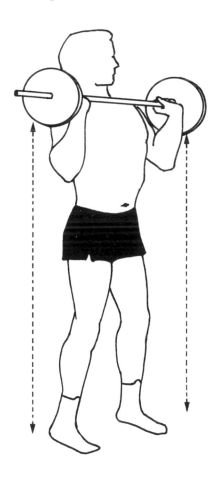

Fig 14 (a) and (b)

Exercise 15 Press with Barbell

From the 'clean' position, which you reached in **Exercise 14**, you press the barbell to arm's length above the head. Press slowly and lower slowly to the clean position again, breathing out as you press it up and in as you lower it. Up and down count as one repetition. This is good for the arms, but also for the back and chest. It mainly benefits the triceps and deltoids.

Exercise 16 Curls with Barbell

Take the bar in both hands, palms upwards, and let it hang at arm's length down in front of you. Your feet are normal distance apart, your hands shoulder width. From this position bring the bar up to your chest by bending your arms. Perform the movement slowly. Breathe out as you raise the bar and in again as you lower it to the position at arm's length.

Quite obviously this movement benefits the biceps.

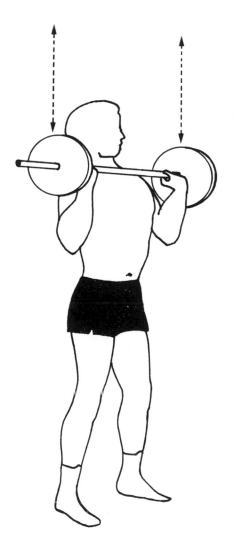

Fig 15

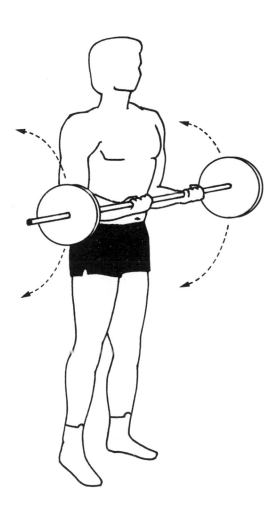

Fig 16

Exercise 17 Reverse Curls with Barbell
For this you will need very light weights. In the beginning you may find it is sufficient to use the bar alone, without weights on it. Hold the bar behind your body with both hands, palms to the front, so that it rests across your buttocks or the tops of your legs. Keeping the body upright, take the bar back as far as it will go. This will be only a few inches, so do not lean forwards to make it more. Having reached that position, turn your wrists back so as to raise the bar a further inch or so. Return to normal, with the bar touching your body. Breathe out as you do the exercise and in as you return to normal. The movement uses the triceps.

Exercise 18 Triceps Stretch Standing
Load the dumb-bell centrally, with a collar each side to hold the weights in position. Hold in both hands above the head, with knuckles to the front, palms to the rear. By bending the elbows, lower the dumb-bell behind the head and bring it back up to the overhead position again. The upper arms remain straight and upright. Breathe in as you lower, out as you raise. This exercise is for the triceps.

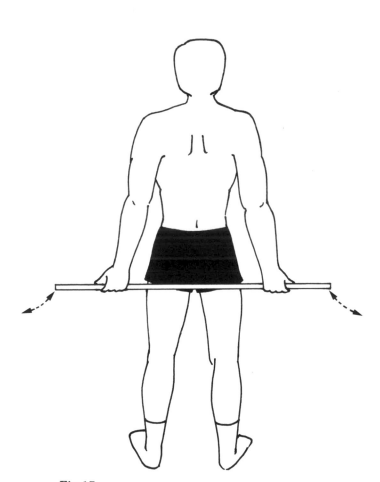

Fig 17

Fig 18

Exercise 19 Triceps Stretch Seated
Take the dumb-bell in your right hand, sit on a bench. Raise the dumb-bell to arm's length overhead, knuckles to the front, palm to the rear. Support your upper arm with your left hand. Lower the dumb-bell behind you by bending your right elbow, maintaining the upper arm vertical. Raise the dumb-bell to arm's length again. Breathe in as you lower it, out as you raise it.

This is another exercise for the triceps. Having used your right hand for one whole set of repetitions, change hands and repeat with your left. Note in this case that the dumb-bell is not loaded centrally, but at each end and you grip it in the centre.

Exercise 20 Single Arm Dumb-bell Curls
Take a loaded dumb-bell in the left hand, palm upwards. Let it hang down at arm's length in front of you, as you stand with feet normal distance apart. Bring it to your shoulder by bending your left elbow. Breathe out as you bring it up, in as you lower again to arm's length. It helps to keep the other hand either at your side, or to take it behind your back as shown in Figure 20. Repeat the exercise with the right hand when you have finished one set of repetitions with the left hand.

The exercise benefits the biceps when you take the dumb-bell up and the triceps as you lower it, providing you control the movement.

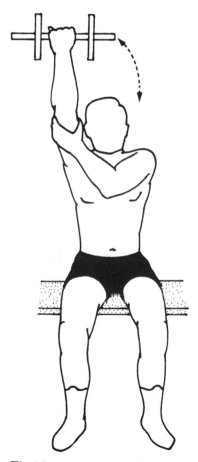

Fig 19

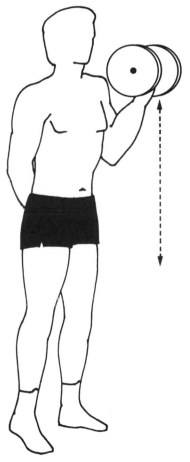

Fig 20

Exercise 21 Press behind Neck with Barbell

Load the barbell. Bring it to the 'clean' position, as in **Exercise 14**, and take it on up over the head to rest on the back of the neck. You may need a slightly wider grip with the hands to do this. The palms are to the front. The fingers curl over the top of the bar. From this position behind the neck, press upwards to arm's length, breathing out as you do so, and return to the position with the bar resting on the back of the neck, breathing in as you do this.

This is very good for the triceps but also benefits the erector spinae muscles.

Fig 21

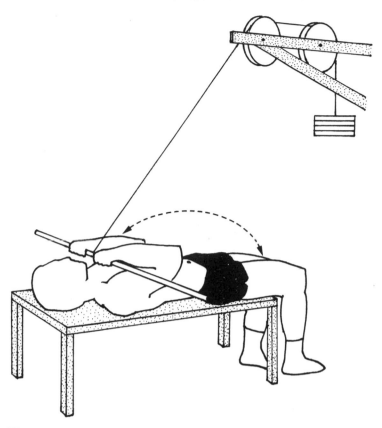

Fig 22

**Exercise 22 Back Lying Curl on Bench
with Pulley and Weights**
Using the pulley system, lie flat on a
bench, take the bar in both hands, with
an underneath grip, knuckles down,
palms up, both feet on the floor. Start
with the bar at arm's length down in
front of you, touching the front of your
thighs. Slowly bring the bar up to your
chest by bending your elbows. Breathe
out as you do this and in as you take it
back to your thighs by straightening
your arms. A grip of shoulder width or
slightly narrower is recommended.

The exercise benefits the biceps and
triceps, and if, when the bar is up to
your chest, you curl your wrists in
towards yourself, it will be an excellent
wrist developer as well.

Exercise 23 Wrist Roller Exercise

For this, we use a piece of apparatus known as a wrist roller. You hold both hands out in front of you palms downwards, holding both ends of the rod and having the weight hanging down at the end of the cord. The exercise consists of raising the weight by twisting the rod and so winding the cord around the rod. It is not only good for the wrists and fingers but for all of the forearm muscles.

Exercise 24 Dumb-bell Raises

Stand normally, feet a comfortable distance apart. Take a dumb-bell in the right hand, with knuckles uppermost, letting it hang down at arm's length in front of you. Keep your other hand by your side. Raise the dumb-bell forwards and upwards keeping your arm straight, until it is level with the shoulder and out at arm's length in front of you. Breathe out as you do so. Lower to the first position, breathing in. Do a set with the right hand, then change hands and do a set with the left. You will use all the arm muscles and the deltoids.

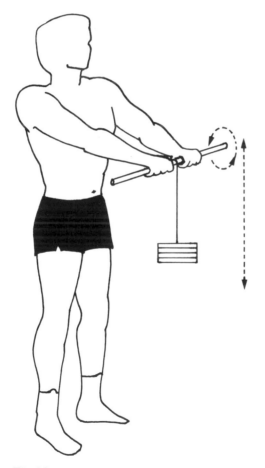

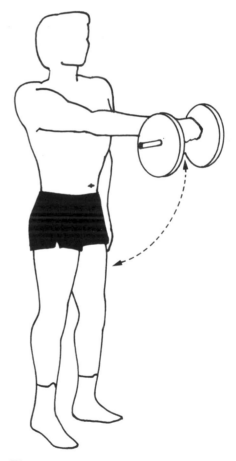

Fig 23

Fig 24

6 Exercises for the Legs

The following exercises principally benefit the legs. Refer to Chapters 9 to 14 for information on how to use them to best advantage.

Exercise 25 Squats with Barbell
Load the barbell, and take it over your head and onto your neck at the back as in **Exercise 21**, palms to the front, fingers over the bar. From this position, do the deep knees bend (see page 60) with the weight on your shoulders. Feet are normal distance apart and heels must remain on the ground. Breathe in as you go down and out as you come up. You may not be able to go right down to begin with, but go as far as you can and try to improve.

For this exercise it will greatly assist to have training partners who can hand you the weight and also take it off your shoulders when you have completed a set. Without them, you have to be able to take it over your head after the last repetition in order to put it down, unless you have squat stands. The use of either squat stands or training partners will enable you to work with a heavier poundage.

Squats are good for the legs but also for the chest because of the deep breathing involved.

There are three variations: **Exercise 25(a) Jumping Squats.** In this, having got down to the deep knees bend position, you spring into an upright position; **Exercise 25(b) Half Squats.** Go down only until the thighs are parallel with the ground and come up again; **Exercise 25(c) Quarter Squats.** Go down just a little way and come up.

Fig 25

Exercise 26 Squats with Barbell at Clean

In the previous exercise, the hands are fairly widely spaced, because the weight is being held at the back of the neck. A variation that allows a narrower grip is the Squat with Barbell at Clean. Here the hands are only shoulder width apart. Take the barbell to the 'clean' position, as described in **Exercise 14**. Do the deep knees bend from this position, breathing in as you go down and out as you come up. Because the weight at the front tends to unbalance you, you will need either shoes with heels, or a block of wood placed under your heels.

This exercise particularly benefits the rectus femoris.

Exercise 27 Straddle Lift

Stand astride the barbell. Feet should be normal distance apart. Grip the bar with one hand in front of the body, palm backwards, the other hand behind the body, palm forwards. Bend the knees to do so and, keeping the trunk upright, lift the bar by straightening the legs. Bend the knees to put it back down again. This exercise can be done with a fairly heavy weight, but start with something you can easily manage. Breathe in as you go down and out as you lift.

The Straddle Lift uses all the leg muscles.

Fig 26

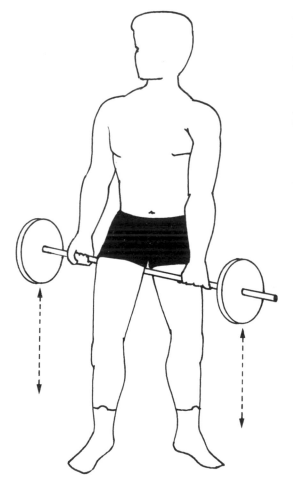

Fig 27

Exercise 28 Heels Raise with Barbell
Take the barbell onto the shoulders behind the neck, in the position shown in **Exercise 21**. The feet should be normal distance apart. With the barbell in this position, raise the heels, holding the position for a moment, before returning the heels to the ground. Breathe out as you raise, in as you lower.

Your lower leg muscles will in particular be exercised and strengthened.

Exercise 29 Seated Heels Raise with Barbell
Sit on a bench, take the loaded barbell across your knees, holding it there with your hands, but letting the full weight rest on your knees. Do the heels raise from this position. If you find it easier, rest the toes on a small block of wood, but this is not essential. Breathe out as you raise, in as you lower. This variation of **Exercise 28** concentrates the work on the calf muscles, and you are able to use a heavier weight so it is particularly beneficial.

Fig 28

Fig 29

Exercise 30 Iron Boots Leg Raise Sideways

For this we need a piece of apparatus known as iron boots.

For the leg raise sideways, stand by a wall. Rest your right hand against the wall, put your left hand on your hip and raise your left leg with the boot on sideways as far as you can, and lower. Do the exercise slowly, breathing out as you raise and in as you lower. Repeat the exercise with the right leg, when you have completed a set with the left.

It is excellent for the tensor muscles, the vastus externus, and indeed for all the leg and hip muscles.

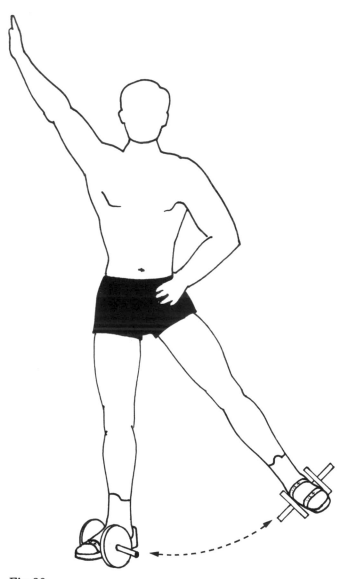

Fig 30

Exercise 31 Iron Boots Leg Raise Backwards

Stand facing a wall and place both hands against it, body upright. Raise your left leg backwards, bending the knee, with the iron boot on. Breathe out as you raise, in as you lower. Having completed a set of repetitions with the left leg, do the same with the right leg.

This exercise is especially beneficial for the muscles at the back of the leg, the biceps of the leg.

Exercise 32 Iron Boots Swing

Stand sideways to a wall, as in **Exercise 30**. Rest your left hand on the wall and your right on your hip. Swing your right foot forwards and backwards with the iron boot on. Change to right hand on wall, left hand on your hip, and swing the left leg forwards and backwards. Keep the leg straight in each case and swing loosely from the hip joint. Exercises the hips and buttocks.

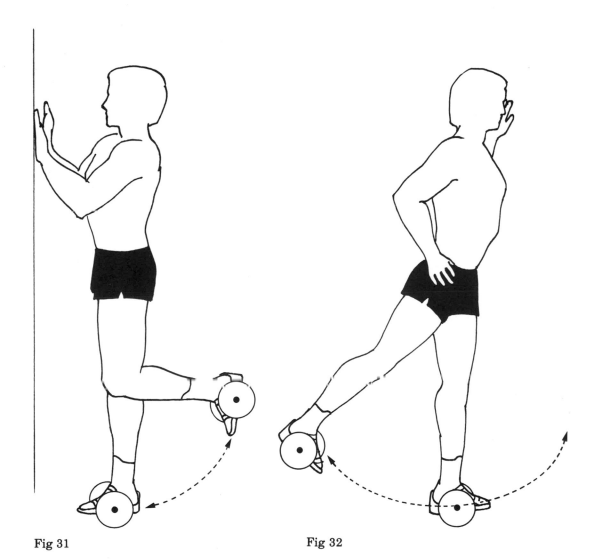

Fig 31   Fig 32

Exercise 33 Iron Boots Knee Raise

Stand with your back to a wall, hands on hips. With iron boots on, raise alternate knees as high as you can in front of you, and lower. Do the exercise slowly and deliberately, breathing out as you raise a knee and in as you lower.

This is excellent for the upper leg muscles and the abdominals, the muscles at the front of the leg being exercised as you raise and those at the back being worked as you lower.

Exercise 34 Iron Boots Thigh Extension

Sit on a bench or table high enough for both legs to hang. Wearing iron boots, alternately raise each leg out straight in front of you to work the leg muscles and also the knee joint.

Exercise 35 Knees Raise with Iron Boots from a Prone Position

Lie on your back, wearing iron boots. Your hands are on the floor at your sides to give you some support. Raise both knees together as high up towards your chest as you can, breathing out as you raise them and in as you take them back to the ground.

As well as benefiting the leg muscles, this is excellent for the abdominals.

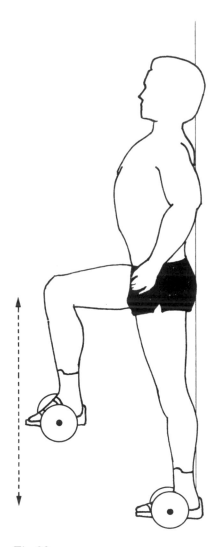

Fig 33

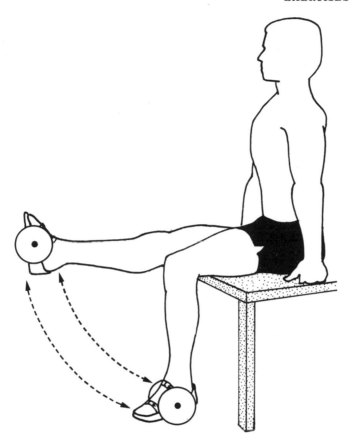

Fig 34

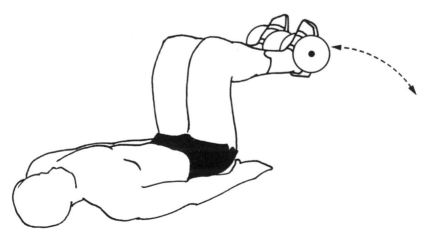

Fig 35

Exercise 36 Legs Raise with Iron Boots from a Prone Position

Lie on your back, wearing iron boots. Your hands are above your head this time. Raise each leg in turn, keeping it straight. Breathe out as you raise and in as you lower. You can vary the exercise by raising both legs at once.

Again, this benefits the leg muscles and the abdominals.

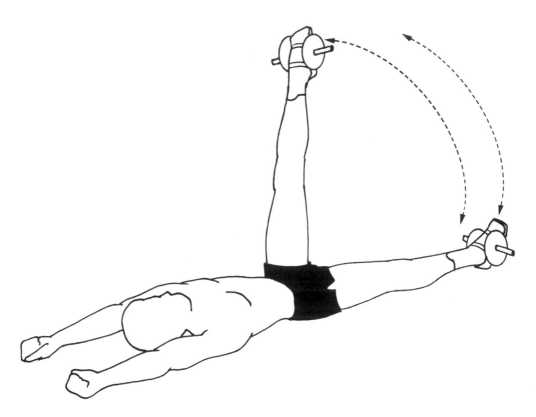

Fig 36

Exercise 37 Leg Presses with Leg-pressing Machine

This exercise uses another piece of apparatus called the Leg-pressing Machine.

To use it, load with a suitable weight, lie on your back. Your legs when placed under the machine at its pegged position are bent. You raise the platform by straightening your legs to full extent, and lower it by bending your knees until it again rests on the pegs. Quite heavy weights can be used in this way, to build massive leg muscles. Breathe out as you press and in as you lower.

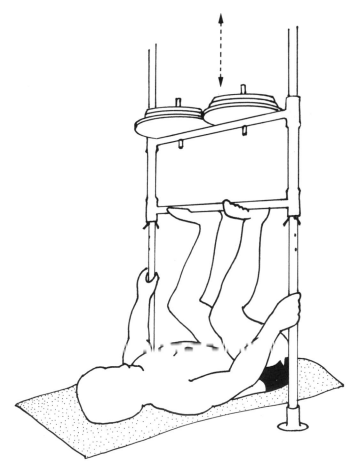

Fig 37

Exercise 38 Heels Raise using Calf Machine

Load with suitable weights and raise the hands to hold the shafts. From this position you do a simple heels raise.

It is a good exercise for the calf muscles, and for the ankle and foot.

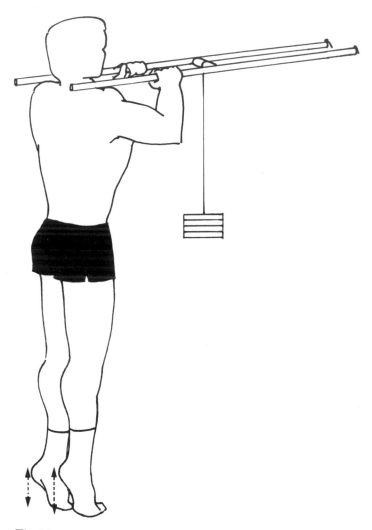

Fig 38

Exercise 39 Step up onto Bench with Weight on Shoulders
Load a barbell with a moderate weight and take it onto the back of the neck as shown in **Exercise 21**. Holding the barbell there and in good balance, step up onto a low bench and down again. Breathe out as you step up and in as you step down.

It will greatly strengthen all the leg muscles, and develop and strengthen the knee joint.

Exercise 40 Hack Lift
Stand with feet normal distance apart in front of a loaded barbell. Bend the knees and, leaning forwards slightly, grasp the barbell with both hands, palms to the front. Lift the barbell by straightening the knees and come to the upright position. Bend the knees to lower the body and replace the barbell on the ground. Breathe out as you lift and in as you lower. This again is good for all the leg muscles.

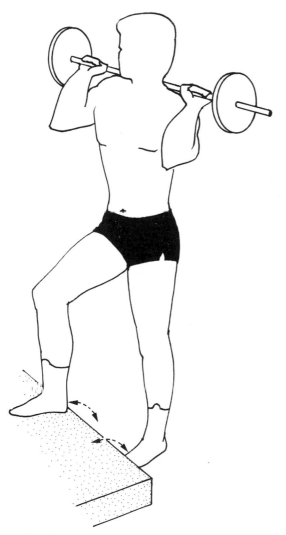

Fig 39

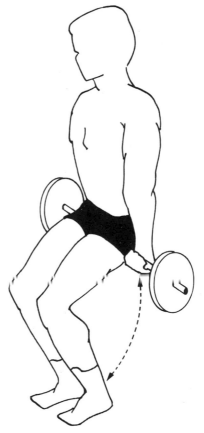

Fig 40

7 Exercises for the Trunk, Neck and Abdomen

As for the previous groups of exercises, refer to Chapters 9 to 14 for information on the use of these exercises and do not simply attempt to do them all at once.

Exercise 41 Good Morning Exercise with Barbell

Take the loaded barbell on the back of the neck as shown in **Exercise 21**. From this position, bend forwards at the waist as far as you can, if possible reaching the position where the chest is at right angles to the legs, but do not lose balance and keep the head well up. Return to the upright position. Breathe out as you go down and in as you come to upright again.

This is an exercise for the trunk and the lower back muscles.

Fig 41

Exercise 42 Exercise with Neck Harness
This piece of apparatus consists of canvas straps, which fit around the forehead and over the top of the head, as in Figure 42. Weights are hung from the straps under the chin.

To use the neck harness, you lean forwards, so that the straps with the weight attached are clear of your body, and simply raise and lower the head. It develops the neck muscles.

Exercise 43 Sit-ups with Weight
Take one of your round disc weights and hold it behind your head with both hands. Lie flat on the floor. Anchor your feet under a loaded barbell so that they will not come up. From this position, sit up, pulling on the weight at the back of your neck to keep it in contact with your head. It is the simple sit-up exercise made harder by the extra weight you are bringing up, and is a very strong abdominal exercise. Breathe out as you sit up and in as you lower yourself back to the floor. Control the lowering as much as the sitting up and do not simply flop back. The upper abdominals benefit most.

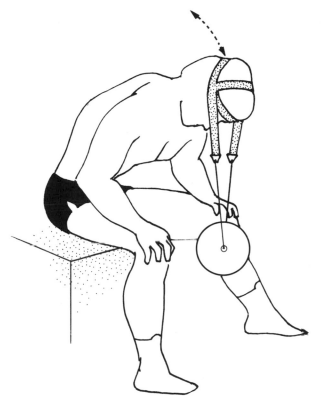

Fig 42

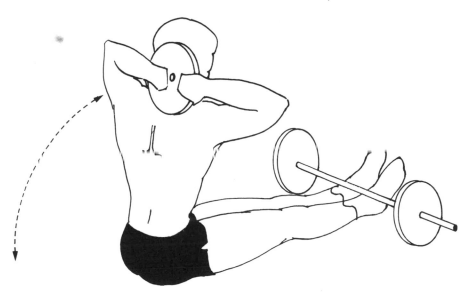

Fig 43

Exercise 44 Legs Raise with Iron Boots using a Beam

Gyms will have beams adjustable to different heights, or even wall bars would be suitable for this exercise, but any beam in a garage or loft will do.

Wearing iron boots, hang from the beam with both hands. Raise both legs to the horizontal position. Breathe out as you raise and in as you lower. This is an exercise for the lower abdominal muscles.

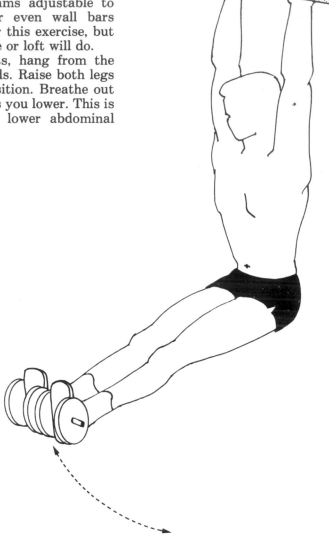

Fig 44

Exercise 45 Legs Raise on Bench with Iron Boots

Wearing iron boots, lie on a bench with your legs projecting over the end and your buttocks just on the bench. Grip the sides of the bench with both hands. Take both your legs up to a position horizontal to the ground and at the level of the bench. This is the starting point. From here, do a double legs raise, taking them as far over your body or head as possible, and return to the position straight out over the end of the bench. Do not put your feet back on the ground between repetitions. Breathe out as you raise the legs, in as you lower. This is one of the most powerful exercises for the lower abdominals.

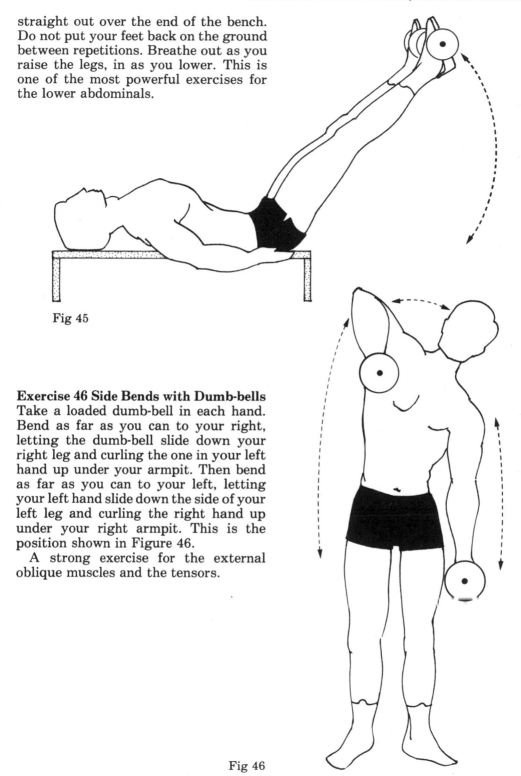

Fig 45

Exercise 46 Side Bends with Dumb-bells
Take a loaded dumb-bell in each hand. Bend as far as you can to your right, letting the dumb-bell slide down your right leg and curling the one in your left hand up under your armpit. Then bend as far as you can to your left, letting your left hand slide down the side of your left leg and curling the right hand up under your right armpit. This is the position shown in Figure 46.

A strong exercise for the external oblique muscles and the tensors.

Fig 46

55

Exercise 47 Trunk Turning with Dumb-bells

Stand feet astride. Take a loaded dumb-bell in each hand and hold arms out in line with the shoulders. Try to keep the hips steady and to turn from the waist to your right as far as you can, turning your head and taking your right arm back and your left forwards so that your arms holding the dumb-bells form a straight line with your shoulders and chest. Turn to face front again and continue round to your left as far as you can. Then back to the front. The trunk muscles will benefit.

Fig 47

Exercise 48 Squats with Dumb-bells at Shoulder

Take a loaded dumb-bell in each hand and bring it to your shoulder. With the dumb-bells held in this position, do a deep knees bend and come up again, maintaining the dumb-bells in the same position throughout the exercise. Breathe in as you go down and out as you come up.

This is a leg exercise as well, of course, but the effort of holding the dumb-bells up and the breathing benefits the upper body too.

Exercise 49 Trunk Turning with Bar across Shoulders

Take a loaded bar to the position behind the neck described in **Exercise 21**. The feet are normal distance apart. From this position, keeping the hips steady, turn from the waist as far to your right as possible, letting the head turn and the bar follow in line with your shoulders. Return to face front and then turn round to your left as far as possible. The bar keeps the shoulders and arms in line.

This exercise uses the muscles around the hips and down the sides of the body.

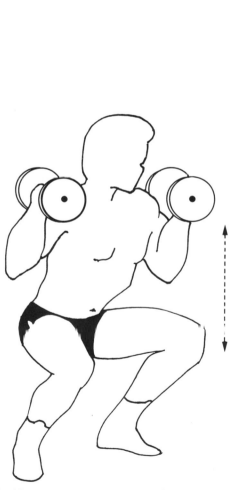

Fig 48

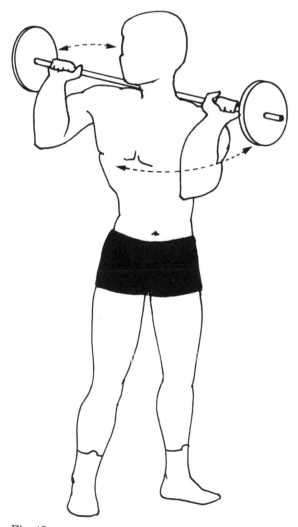

Fig 49

Exercise 50 Sit-ups on Incline Bench with Weight

The incline bench can be set to any angle. Make it about 30° to the horizontal to begin with. At the top there is a strap under which you can put your feet to hold them. See that it is secure. Lie head downwards and taking a round disc weight, hold it at the back of your neck and head with both hands. Now do sit-ups. Breathe in as you go back down and out as you sit up. The exercise can be made progressive in two ways. Either you can add to the weight, or you can increase the angle of the bench. Or, of course, you can do both, though there is a limit to the angle to which you can raise the bench without slipping off.

This is a strong abdominal exercise.

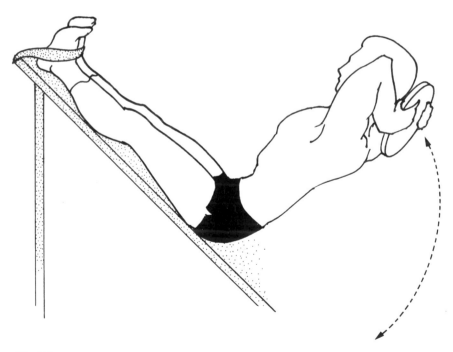

Fig 50

Exercise 51 Side Bends with Dumb-bells over Head

Load the dumb-bell centrally. Grasp it on either side, with hands straight up above your head. Your fingers curl over the top of the rod, your palms to the front. Stand with feet normal distance apart. Bend as far as you can to your left and then straighten up and bend as far as you can to your right.

This is one of the strongest exercises for the muscles of the trunk.

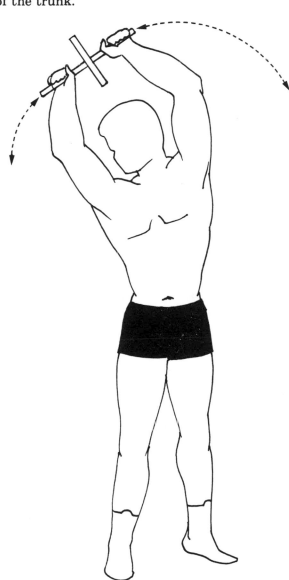

Fig 51

8 Free-standing Warming-up Exercises

It is unwise to go straight into any strenuous activity while the body and the muscles are cold. This can lead to strains. Before starting any training programme, therefore, do a few warming-up exercises without apparatus.

The exercises given below should warm up all your limbs and enable you to go on safely to your training programme with weights. Train in a comfortably warm room, however, and out of draughts. If you are wearing minimal clothing, as is best, put on a sweater or track suit jacket between sets of an exercise. Do not chill off during your training session.

As well as warming up you should relax at the end and there is nothing like deep breathing for this. After your weight session, therefore, repeat **Exercises 59 and 60.**

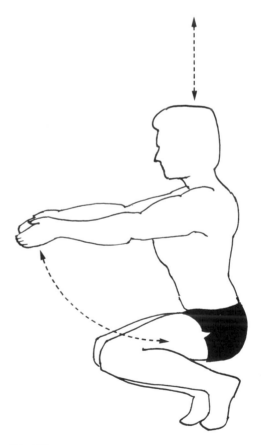

Exercise 52 Deep Knees Bends
Stand upright, head erect, shoulders back and relaxed, feet normal distance apart and arms hanging at the sides. Rise on the toes and do a deep knees bend, at the same time swinging your arms forwards to shoulder level, to help maintain your balance. Try to go down as far as you can and to sit on your heels. Breathe in deeply as you go down and out again as you come up. Let your arms drop back down as you come up. Do 10 repetitions.

Fig 52

Exercise 53 Touching Floor between Legs
Stand with the feet astride. Take the arms above your head and back. Breathe in deeply. Bend forwards and touch the floor between your legs, breathing out as you go down and in as you come back up. Do 10 repetitions.

Figs 53 (a) and (b)

Exercise 54 Trunk Turning
Stand upright, feet apart, arms stretched out sideways at shoulder level as far as you can. Try to keep the hips still and to turn the trunk as far as you can to your right. Turn your head to look to your right rear and your trunk will follow. Come back to the front and turn to the left. Perform the movement rhythmically with a swing. Do 10 turns each way.

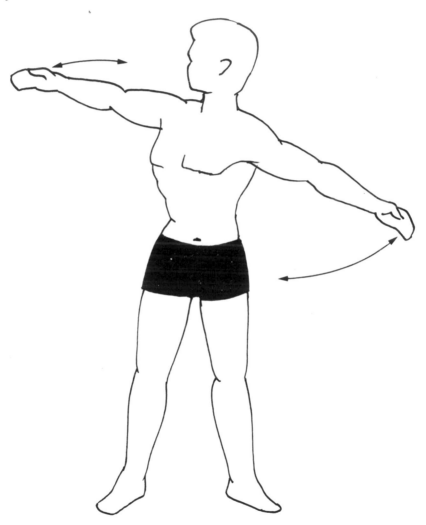

Fig 54

Exercise 55 Side Bends

Stand upright, feet together, hands at sides, palms inwards. Keep the body facing to the front and bend over to your right as far as you can, letting your hand slide down the side of your leg. Try to reach down as far as possible with the fingertips. Straighten up and bend over to the left as far as possible in the same way. Do 10 bends each side.

Exercise 56 Head Circling

Stand upright, hands at sides, feet together. Bend the head forwards as far as possible, take it to your right shoulder, then up and back, then to your left, forwards to your left shoulder to the centre again, moving it round in a circle anti-clockwise. Do 5 circles and then repeat in a clockwise direction. Do 5 repetitions each way.

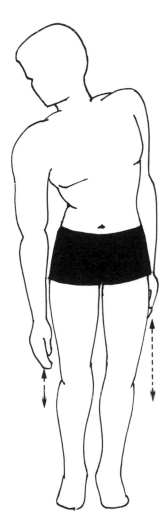

Fig 55

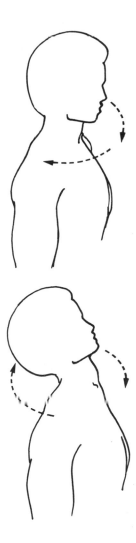

Fig 56

Exercise 57 Skipping
Take a skipping rope and skip for 30
seconds, counting them. An alternative
is running on the spot.

Exercise 58 Touching Alternate Toes
Stand with feet astride, arms raised
above the head. Bend forwards and with
the right fingertips try to touch the left
toes. Straighten up, and with the left
fingertips try to touch the right toes.
Breathe out as you bend down and in as
you straighten up. Do 10 with each
hand.

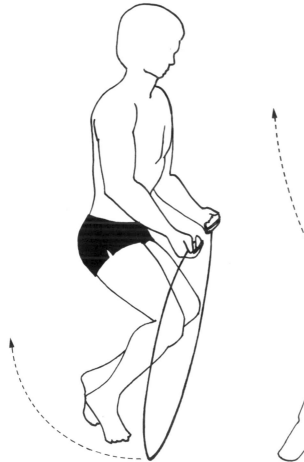

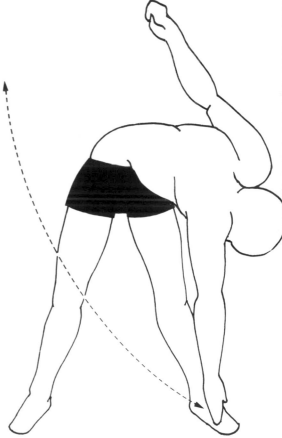

Fig 57

Fig 58

Exercise 59 Deep Breathing with Arms Swinging

Stand upright and relaxed, head up and shoulders back. Cross the arms in front of you. Swing the arms upwards sideways and back, as you breathe in deeply. Breathe out, bringing the arms down to the crossed position in front of you again. Do 10 repetitions.

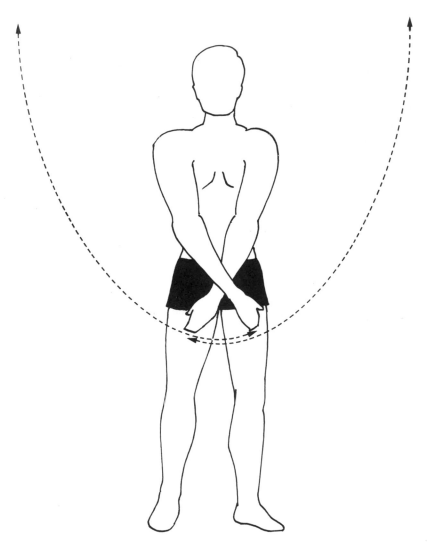

Fig 59

Exercise 60 Relaxing

Stand upright. Let the arms hang loosely at your sides, and shake each in turn, being sure to let the wrist relax as well, and to shake that. Think of your arm as a rope hanging loosely from your shoulder, not stiff at all, and shake it for 10 seconds. Repeat with the other arm.

Raise one leg off the ground and, letting it hang loosely as you did the arm, shake it gently for 10 seconds, letting it swing. Repeat with the other leg.

This last exercise is rarely met with in weight training or body building courses and it is interesting to know that it forms part of the warming-up exercises in karate, where it has been found beneficial in preparing the muscles and limbs for the more intensive training movements that follow.

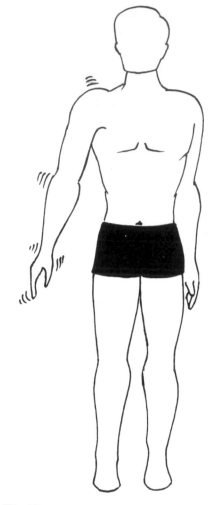

Fig 60

9 A Simple Keep Fit Scheme

Not everyone has the time or the interest to seriously set about developing his or her physique, but a sensible person obviously wants to keep fit. Some take up jogging or cycling or some other sport, but the drawback to most of these activities is that they exercise one particular muscle group more than others. What you need for fitness is all-round exercise that uses every muscle group in the body and for this purpose weight training is ideal.

If development is your aim, refer to Chapter 10, and modify the schemes there to meet your need. If all you want is fitness, then follow the course in this chapter. It is necessary to do only one set of each exercise, not two or three as for development, since all you want to do is to work each group of muscles, not to exhaust them. A simple keep fit scheme can be followed every day. The first time you try it, your muscles will be aching afterwards and you will still feel the effects the next day. Do not give up. In a week or so, you will be able to follow your schedule quite easily and it will keep you in trim for the rest of your life.

In order to stay encouraged to keep it up, it is best not to overload yourself with work, so I have chosen only eight exercises in addition to the warm up and the relaxing at the end.

Your course is as follows:

Without any weights at all, do the free-standing warming-up exercises in Chapter 8 **Exercises 52 to 60**. This is preparatory work.

Then, with weights:

Exercise 25 Squats with Barbell.

Exercise 16 Curls with Barbell.
Exercise 17 Reverse Curls with Barbell.
Exercise 15 Press with Barbell.
Exercise 1 Bent Over Rowing.
Exercise 43 Sit-ups with Weight.
Exercise 45 Legs Raise on Bench.
(NB: This is described with iron boots. If you do not have this piece of apparatus, do twice as many repetitions without.)
Exercise 3 Bench Press.
Finish with a repeat of **Exercises 59 and 60**.

For this routine, use fairly light weights, choosing a poundage that enables you to do ten repetitions without straining on the last. Do ten repetitions of each exercise, except where more is indicated. The complete schedule should not take you more than thirty minutes, possibly less.

Should you find after a few months that it is becoming too easy, add a little more weight, say 5lb, rather than increase the number of repetitions, as the latter will quickly bring you to a point where the course is taking too long to complete and absorbing too much of your time. You can spare half an hour a day for fitness. You are unlikely to spare an hour or an hour-and-a-half for more than a very limited period.

One of the problems you will have to overcome is boredom with doing the same exercises all the time. The best way to do this is to introduce variations. Assuming you have only a barbell and dumb-bells and an ordinary bench, you can substitute as follows:

For **Exercise 25** Squats with Barbell, do **Exercise 26** Squats with Barbell at Clean, or **Exercise 48** Squats with Dumb-bells at Shoulder.

For **Exercise 16** Curls with Barbell, do **Exercise 20** Single Arm Dumb-bell Curls.

For **Exercise 17** Reverse Curls with Barbell, do **Exercise 18** Triceps Stretch Standing, or **Exercise 19** Triceps Stretch Seated using dumb-bells.

For **Exercise 15** Press with Barbell, do **Exercise 21** Press behind Neck with Barbell, or **Exercise 7** Alternate Dumb-bell Presses.

For **Exercise 1** Bent Over Rowing, do **Exercise 10** Single Hand Rowing.

For **Exercise 43** Sit-ups with Weight, try **Exercise 50** Sit-ups on Incline Bench if you have a bench.

For **Exercise 45** Legs Raise on Bench, try **Exercise 44** Leg Raises using a Beam, using iron boots if you have them.

For **Exercise 3** Bench Press, do **Exercise 4** Crucifix with Dumb-bells.

Occasionally, if you wish, leave out one of the exercises, and try one from the same group for a week or two, but do not make the mistake of always leaving out the exercises you find hardest. It is the ones you find hardest that you most need. If you have pulley and weights, or wrist roller, or head harness, or a calf machine or a leg pressing machine, you will easily see what exercises use of these will replace. But such equipment is quite unnecessary for an ordinary keep fit course. It is more the kind of thing serious body builders would go in for.

10 Body Building

Body building is a wide term and can mean everything from correcting under-development to building your physique up to championship standard. Most people are content with the first aim, but for those who wish to go further, it is only a question of doing more, not of doing something different.

If you wish to go in for championships, there are regional and national competitions, culminating in the Mr Universe event, and you would be well advised to join the national organis-ation, the National Amateur Body Builders Association. There is much that only a personal instructor could teach you about posing, muscle control and showmanship. In this book, we are concerned only with the exercises required for development.

The first thing to realise is that muscles do not grow in a day or even a month. You must be prepared for patient effort over a period of at least two years. I have accordingly planned a two-year course. Naturally, you can go on even further, and if you have not achieved your ideal by then, you will have to do so, but two years should see such a dramatic difference, particularly if you are thin and underdeveloped to begin with, that you will need no persuasion to carry on.

You can work with only a barbell, two dumb-bells and a bench, which can be the simplest flat bench, and I have given a course that can be done with just these pieces of apparatus. Other equipment does not make for better results; it simply enables you to add variety to your work-outs, and this is explained in

the appropriate places. You could, of course, do the exercises you started with right through the two-year period, simply adding to the weight you were using, but since this becomes rather boring, the exercises in this course change every two months, so that you will have variety.

First of all decide which body type you are (see page 14), so that you make the adjustments to the weight used according to your type. Take all your measurements to begin with and record them together with your weight, as suggested in Chapter 2. You should, of course, always measure before exercising and take your weight first thing in the morning before you dress. Do not be distressed if your measure-ments show a decrease in the first month or two, as it is not unusual to lose fat before building muscle in its place. Measure every month and keep a record.

Work out the weight you are going to use for each exercise before you begin (see page 15) and make a note of it, also noting when you increase the weight you are using. As already mentioned, the small-boned man should start with 00 per cent of the weight he could lift just once in a particular exercise; the medium man should deduct 5lb from this; and the heavy big man should deduct 10lb. It should be made clear that here we are talking of the major lifting exercises such as the press, the bench press, curls, squats, etc. With iron boots, dumb-bells and so on, your starting weight would probably be too little for these adjustments to be made, so just use a little less weight if you are the medium or the big man. When you train, have your records before you, so that you can quickly change discs on your bars, without relying on memory.

Always begin with free-standing warming-up exercises; always finish with deep breathing and relaxing. Train three nights a week, with a night's rest in between. Thus, your programme can be Mondays, Wednesdays and Fridays, or Tuesdays, Thursdays and Saturdays, but not both. There must be the rest period of forty-eight hours between each work-out.

If you have never done any training before, follow the special introductory schedule for the first month. If you have some experience or are fit and used to sports and games, you can omit this and start with the schedule for Month Two.

If you have any physical ailment at all or suspect any defect in your body, such as a weak heart or asthma, consult your doctor before embarking on any course, and abide by his decision. Providing you are in normal health, however, you can go ahead without fear.

The training session will be divided into six parts: warming-up, exercises for the legs, exercises for the arms, exercises for the upper body, exercises for the abdominal muscles, relaxing, so that at each session you will cover every major muscle group and so bring about all-round and proportional development.

Month One
For the complete beginner, use 60 per cent of the maximum weight you could lift on any exercise.
To warm up **Exercises 52 to 60.**
Exercise 25 Squats with Barbell. 2 sets of 8 repetitions only.
Exercise 16 Curls with Barbell. 2 sets of 8 repetitions only.
Exercise 18 Triceps Stretch Standing. 2 sets of 8 repetitions only.
Exercise 15 Press with Barbell. 2 sets of 8 repetitions only.
Exercise 1 Bent Over Rowing. 2 sets of 8 repetitions only.
Exercise 5 Straight Arm Pullovers. 2

sets of 8 repetitions only.
Exercise 43 Sit-ups, but without the weight. 2 sets of 8 repetitions only.
Exercise 36 Legs Raise from a Prone Position, but without using iron boots. 2 sets of 10 repetitions only.
Exercise 46 Side Bends with Dumbbells. Use not more than 10lb on dumbbells and do 2 sets of 10 repetitions only.
Exercise 47 Trunk Turning with Dumbbells. Use not more than 10lb on dumbbells and do 2 sets of 10 repetitions only.
To relax **Exercises 59 and 60.**

If you are experienced or athletic and would find this too easy, go straight into Month Two, and follow it for the first two months.

Month Two
Use 60 per cent of the maximum weight you could handle once in any exercise; do two sets to the point of resistance, that is until you try the exercise but just cannot manage the lift. It is the one that you just cannot manage that does all the good; the preceding ones are just bringing your body to this point.
To warm up **Exercises 52 to 60.**
Exercise 25 Squats with Barbell. 2 sets. You will probably find that you can manage 10 repetitions on the first set. Have a minute's rest and you may be able to do 8 on the second set. When the number you can do on the first set increases to above 13, then add a little weight, so as to bring it back down again to around about 10. This applies to all the lifting exercises or those in which heavy weights are used.
Exercise 16 Curls with Barbell. 2 sets. Again 10 repetitions in the first set and 8 in the second would be reasonable for a beginner.
Exercise 18 Triceps Stretch Standing. 2 sets. 10 and 8 would be a reasonable number at this stage.
Exercise 15 Press with Barbell. 2 sets. 10 and 8 would be a reasonable performance.
Exercise 1 Bent Over Rowing. 2 sets. 10 and 8 would be reasonable.

Exercise 5 Straight Arm Pullovers. 2 sets. This will be harder, and 10 would be good for the first attempt.

Exercise 43 Sit-ups. Do without weight at this stage. 2 sets. 15 to 20 in the first and 12 to 15 in the second would be about average.

Exercise 36 Legs Raise from a Prone Position. Do without the iron boots at this stage. 2 sets. 20 each leg, followed by 15 each leg would be average. Do each raise slowly and control the lowering.

Exercise 46 Side Bends with Dumb-bells. 2 sets. 15 each side followed by 12 each side would be average.

Exercise 47 Trunk Turning with Dumb-bells. Keep your arms up, as the heavy weights will make them sag. 2 sets. 15 turns each way per set.

To relax **Exercises 59 and 60**.

Make sure you are taking a minute's rest between each set and also between each exercise, but not, of course, between each repetition. I have gone into details of what you could expect to be doing in this month's schedule. If you can do more, so much the better; if less, you will work up to these numbers in time, so do not worry. The main thing to remember is to add weights whenever your first set increases to more than thirteen repetitions, otherwise you will quickly find yourself doing a vast number and you will not have time to complete your work-out. Estimated performance is not given for the rest of the course, as it will vary so much with the individual and the progress he is making that it would be pure guesswork and no real help as a guide.

Months Three and Four
To warm up **Exercises 52 to 60**.
Exercise 25 Squats with Barbell. 2 sets.
Exercise 20 Single Arm Dumb-bell Curls. 2 sets.
Exercise 19 Triceps Stretch Seated. 2 sets.
Exercise 21 Press behind Neck with Barbell. 2 sets.

Exercise 2 Upright Rowing. 2 sets.
Exercise 6 Bent Arm Pullovers. 2 sets.
Exercise 43 Sit-ups with Weight. Try it with 15lb. 2 sets.
Exercise 36 Legs Raise with Iron Boots from a Prone Position. Try it with boots only and no extra weight added. 2 sets.
Exercise 46 Side Bends with Dumb-bells. 2 sets.
Exercise 49 Trunk Turning with Bar across Shoulders. Try it with bar only and no weight. 1 set of 20 turns each way.

To relax **Exercises 59 and 60**.

Breathing is most important in all these exercises and will greatly develop your chest, which is made bigger first by expanding the lung capacity and then by building the muscles around it, such as the pectorals.

Months Five and Six
To warm up **Exercises 52 to 60**.
Exercise 26 Squats with Barbell at Clean. 3 sets this month.
Exercise 22 Back Lying Curl on Bench with Pulley with Weights. 3 sets (If you have no pulley do **Exercise 16** instead, Curls with Barbell.)
Exercise 8 Lateral Raises. 3 sets.
Exercise 14 Clean with Barbell. 3 sets.
Exercise 7 Alternate Dumb-bell Presses. 3 sets.
Exercise 43 Sit-ups with Weight. Try 20lb. 3 sets.
Exercise 36 Legs Raise with Iron Boots from a Prone Position. Try it with boots only. 3 sets.
Exercise 46 Side Bends with Dumb-bells. 3 sets.
Exercise 49 Trunk Turning with Bar across Shoulders. Put 20lb on bar and do 3 sets of 20 turns each way.

To relax **Exercises 59 and 60**.

Months Seven and Eight
We are making considerable changes with the exercises this period to give you variety, but all muscle groups will still be used.

To warm up **Exercise 52 to 60**.

Exercise 27 Straddle Lift. 3 sets with the heaviest weight you can manage and still achieve 10 repetitions on the first set.
Exercise 3 Bench Press. 3 sets.
Exercise 4 Crucifix with Dumb-bells. 3 sets.
Exercise 9 Forward and Upward Swing with Dumb-bells. 3 sets.
Exercise 10 Single Hand Rowing. 3 sets each hand.
Exercise 50 Sit-ups on Incline Bench with Weight. Try 25lb. 3 sets.
Exercise 45 Legs Raise on Bench with Iron Boots. 3 sets with boots only.
Exercise 47 Trunk Turning with Dumb-bells. 3 sets of 20 each way with 10lb dumb-bells.
Exercise 46 Side Bends with Dumb-bells. 3 sets.
Exercise 28 Heels Raise with Barbell. 3 sets. Use a weight that enables you to do 10 repetitions on the first set.
To relax **Exercises 59 and 60.**

Months Nine and Ten
Again, we have variety.
To warm up **Exercises 52 to 60.**
Exercise 48 Squats with Dumb-bells at Shoulder. 3 sets with as heavy a weight as you can manage.
Exercise 15 Press with Barbell. 3 sets.
Exercise 17 Reverse Curls with Barbell. 3 sets. Either use the bar alone, or if you can manage it a light weight, say 5lb.
Exercise 16 Curls with Barbell. 3 sets.
Exercise 24 Dumb-bell Raises. 3 sets.
Exercise 23 Wrist Roller Exercise. Use a weight of 10lb and try rolling it up 3 times.
Exercise 29 Seated Heels Raise with Barbell. 3 sets.
Exercise 47 Trunk Turning with Dumb-bells. 3 sets of 20 each way with 15lb dumb-bells.
Exercise 46 Side Bends with Dumb-bells. 3 sets.
Exercise 45 Legs Raise on Bench with Iron Boots. 3 sets, with boots only.
Exercise 50 Sit-ups on Incline Bench with Weight. 3 sets with 25lb.
To relax **Exercises 59 and 60.**

Months Eleven and Twelve
To complete the first year, we are going back to the first month's session, but you will now be using much heavier weights and will be doing three sets instead of two, so you will easily see the progress you have made in the year. Poundages that seemed impossible to you in the beginning will now be taken in your stride.
To warm up **Exercises 52 to 60.**
Exercise 25 Squats with Barbell. 3 sets.
Exercise 16 Curls with Barbell. 3 sets.
Exercise 18 Triceps Stretch Standing. 3 sets.
Exercise 15 Press with Barbell. 3 sets.
Exercise 1 Bent Over Rowing. 3 sets.
Exercise 5 Straight Arm Pullovers. 3 sets.
Exercise 43 Sit-ups with Weight. 3 sets with as much weight as you can manage.
Exercise 36 Legs Raise with Iron Boots from a Prone Position. 3 sets with weights on the boots if you can manage it.
Exercise 46 Side Bends with Dumb-bells. 3 sets.
Exercise 47 Trunk Turning with Dumb-bells. 3 sets of 20 each way.
To relax **Exercises 59 and 60.**

It would not be a bad idea to take a rest from training at the end of the first year, for about a fortnight, during which you do only the free-standing warming-up exercises to keep you supple. You will return refreshed to the second year and will certainly see substantial increases in your measurements by now.

Months Thirteen and Fourteen
To warm up **Exercises 52 to 60.**
Exercise 25 Squats with Barbell. 3 sets.
Exercise 16 Curls with Barbell. 3 sets.
Exercise 17 Reverse Curls with Barbell. 3 sets. You should be able to use some weight on the bar now.
Exercise 15 Press with Barbell. 3 sets.
Exercise 3 Bench Press. 3 sets.
Exercise 10 Single Hand Rowing. 3 sets.
Exercise 39 Step up onto Bench with Weight on Shoulders. Do 1 set of 20,

using a weight that enables you to complete this set.

Exercise 40 Hack Lift. 3 sets.

Exercise 42 Exercise with Neck Harness. 1 set with a 10lb weight.

Exercise 46 Side Bends with Dumbbells. 3 sets.

Exercise 47 Trunk Turning with Dumbbells. 3 sets of 20 each way.

Exercise 50 Sit-ups on Incline Bench with Weight. 3 sets with 25lb.

Exercise 45 Legs Raise on Bench with Iron Boots. 3 sets with weights if you can manage it.

To relax **Exercises 59 and 60**.

Months Fifteen and Sixteen

Again, new exercises are introduced, if you have the apparatus; alternatives are given if you have not.

To warm up **Exercises 52 to 60**.

If you have a pulley and weights:

Exercise 11 Pull to Chest using Pulley and Weights. 3 sets.

Exercise 12 Pull to Back of Neck using Pulley and Weights. 3 sets.

Exercise 13 Pull to Chest on Incline Bench. 3 sets.

If you do not have this apparatus, do the following three exercises instead:

Exercise 1 Bent Over Rowing. 3 sets.

Exercise 21 Press behind Neck with Barbell. 3 sets.

Exercise 16 Curls with Barbell. 3 sets.

Then go on to:

Exercise 30 Iron Boots Leg Raise Sideways. 3 sets with boots only.

Exercise 31 Iron Boots Leg Raise Backwards. 3 sets with boots only.

Exercise 32 Iron Boots Swing. 10 swings each leg, with boots only.

Exercise 33 Iron Boots Knee Raise. 3 sets with boots only.

Exercise 34 Iron Boots Thigh Extension. 3 sets with boots only.

Exercise 41 Good Morning Exercise with Barbell. 3 sets.

Exercise 51 Side Bends with Dumb-bell over Head. 3 sets of 20 each side, with dumb-bell light enough to manage this.

To relax **Exercises 59 and 60**.

In the latter part of this period, you can add a small weight to the iron boots, if you find it too easy without.

Months Seventeen and Eighteen

To warm up **Exercises 52 to 60**.

If you have a leg pressing machine:

Exercise 37 Leg Presses with Leg-pressing Machine. 3 sets.

If not, do:

Exercise 25 Squats with Barbell. 3 sets.

If you have a calf machine:

Exercise 38 Heels Raise using Calf Machine. 3 sets.

If not, do:

Exercise 39 Step up onto Bench with Weight on Shoulders. 3 sets.

If you have a beam:

Exercise 44 Legs Raise with Iron Boots using a Beam. 3 sets.

If not, do:

Exercise 45 Legs Raise on Bench with Iron Boots. 3 sets.

Then continue with:

Exercise 2 Upright Rowing. 3 sets.

Exercise 15 Press with Barbell. 3 sets.

Exercise 17 Reverse Curls with Barbell. 3 sets.

Exercise 3 Bench Press. 3 sets.

Exercise 46 Side Bends with Dumbbells. 3 sets.

Exercise 49 Trunk Turning with Bar across Shoulders. Put 25lb on the bar and do 1 set of 20 turns each way.

Exercise 43 Sit-ups with Weight. 3 sets with as much weight as you can manage.

Exercise 35 Knees Raise with Iron Boots from a Prone Position. 3 sets with as much weight as you can manage.

To relax **Exercises 59 and 60**.

Months Nineteen and Twenty

For the rest of the course, we are going back to earlier routines but working four sets instead of three.

To warm up **Exercises 52 to 60**.

Exercise 25 Squats with Barbell. 4 sets. You might manage something like 10, 8, 7 and 5 or 6 repetitions. Change the poundage when your first set reaches 13.

Exercise 20 Single Arm Dumb-bell Curls. 4 sets.

Exercise 19 Triceps Stretch Seated. 4 sets.
Exercise 21 Press behind Neck with Barbell. 4 sets.
Exercise 2 Upright Rowing. 4 sets.
Exercise 6 Bent Arm Pullovers. 4 sets.
Exercise 43 Sit-ups with Weight. 4 sets with as much weight as you can manage.
Exercise 36 Legs Raise with Iron Boots from a Prone Position. 4 sets with as much weight as you can manage.
Exercise 46 Side Bends with Dumb-bells. 4 sets.
Exercise 49 Trunk Turning with Bar across Shoulders. 4 sets of 20 each way, with as much weight as you can manage.
To relax **Exercises 59 and 60**.

Months Twenty-one and Twenty-two
To warm up **Exercises 52 to 60**.
Exercise 26 Squats with Barbell at Clean. 4 sets.
Exercise 22 Back Lying Curl on Bench with Pulley and Weights. 4 sets. (If you have no pulley, do **Exercise 16** Curls with Barbell, instead. 4 sets.)
Exercise 8 Lateral Raises. 4 sets.
Exercise 14 Clean with Barbell. 4 sets.
Exercise 7 Alternate Dumb-bell Presses. 4 sets.
Exercise 43 Sit-ups with Weight. 4 sets with as much weight as you can manage.
Exercise 36 Legs Raise with Iron Boots from a Prone Position. 4 sets with as much weight as you can manage.
Exercise 46 Side Bends with Dumb-bells. 4 sets.
Exercise 49 Trunk Turning with Bar across Shoulders. 20 turns each way per set. 4 sets with as much weight as you can manage on bar.
To relax **Exercises 59 and 60**.

Months Twenty-three and Twenty-four
To warm up **Exercises 52 to 60**.

Exercise 27 Straddle Lift. 4 sets with as much weight as you can manage.
Exercise 28 Heels Raise with Barbell. 4 sets.
Exercise 3 Bench Press. 4 sets.
Exercise 4 Crucifix with Dumb-bells. 4 sets.
Exercise 7 Alternate Dumb-bell Presses. 4 sets.
Exercise 10 Single Hand Rowing. 4 sets.
Exercise 50 Sit-ups on Incline Bench with Weight. 4 sets.
Exercise 45 Legs Raise on Bench with Iron Boots. 4 sets.
Exercise 47 Trunk Turning with Dumb-bells. 4 sets of 20 each way.
Exercise 46 Side Bends with Dumb-bells.
To relax **Exercises 59 and 60**.

This programme completes a two-year course. You may ask, what now? You will already have achieved considerable progress in building up your physique and strength. To go on, you need to bear two things in mind. First, you must do a balanced work-out each time, covering all the muscle groups, as we have been doing. Secondly, now that you are experienced and fit, consider what extras you want to add to the basic programme for specific development and choose extra exercises accordingly. For example, if you want to develop your legs, add plenty of iron boot work; if your arms, add plenty of curls using all the variations, balancing ordinary curls for the biceps with reverse curls for the triceps. If you want to develop your chest, straight arm pullovers, bench press, crucifix with dumb-bells and so on are what you need. You can now afford to specialise, providing you keep up a basic programme and do not over-exert yourself.

11 Circuit Training

Circuit training is a comparatively new idea in the weight training field. It was first expounded by R. E. Morgan and G. T. Adamson in their book *Circuit Training*, published by G. Bell & Sons Ltd in 1957. Since then, it has become very popular.

Circuit training is training for all-round fitness and stamina rather than for any particular sport but, obviously because of its all-round value, it is of assistance to any sportsman, whatever his speciality. There are many advantages to the system. It has enough variety of exercises to suit everyone and to maintain interest; it does not take much time; and it can be done in a confined space.

The basic idea is this: you have ten exercises and arrange them in such an order that no two similar muscle groups are exercised consecutively. For example, leg exercises must be followed by arm exercises or abdominal exercises. Having chosen your ten exercises, you set up a circuit, with the apparatus laid out ready. Obviously, this is easier to do if you are training in a gym, where everything is to hand, but even if training alone at home, providing you have enough apparatus, you can set up a circuit.

You choose comparatively light weights and, at first, you find your score of how many repetitions you can perform of each exercise in sixty seconds, resting if you have to. You record all these scores. Then you halve them, to get the number of repetitions you are actually going to do.

The training then consists of starting at the beginning of the circuit, going around doing these half numbers of repetitions of the ten exercises, with little or no rest at all. You have to complete the circuit three times without stopping.

You should complete this in thirty minutes for the three rounds. When your time for the circuit is only twenty minutes, you re-test yourself to make it harder, as you did in the beginning, finding out a new total of repetitions for each exercise and halving this. If it is still too easy add some weights to your bars or dumb-bells, but do not work with too heavy weights; 60lb on the bar and 10lb on each dumb-bell will be sufficient. Indeed, the circuit is sometimes set up in a gym entirely with free-standing exercises, but since we are dealing with weight training in this book, we are outlining a weight training circuit.

If you are training in a gym with others, one man starts the circuit and the others follow behind him. If you are working alone at home, you must have sufficient apparatus to lay out ready; there is no time to stop and change weights on a bar. If you do not have enough apparatus for this, it would be better to use what you have for the main exercises and to substitute free-standing exercises for the rest.

If planning your own circuit, bear in mind that circuit training is for the whole body and should not concentrate on one group of muscles rather than another. Most athletes find that it improves stamina. Work on two nights a week when you are not training for other sports and use the circuit instead of the courses in Chapters 12 and 13, not in addition to them. Keep records of your progress.

You can plan your own circuit, but to give an idea of what is wanted, the following sequence is suggested:

Exercise 25 Squats with Barbell.
Exercise 15 Press with Barbell.
Exercise 43 Sit-ups, with or without weight, as you feel able.
Exercise 25(a) Jumping Squats.
Exercise 16 Curls with Barbell.
Exercise 36 Legs Raise, with or without iron boots, as you feel able.
Exercise 2 Upright Rowing.
Exercise 39 Step up onto Bench with Weight on Shoulders.
Exercise 6 Bent Arm Pullovers.
Exercise 35 Knees Raise, with or without iron boots, as you feel able.

You will know enough about weight training at this stage to see that this circuit exercises all your muscles, and that no two similar groups are in sequence.

12 Weight Training for Athletics

In Britain the value of weight training for athletes began to receive official recognition only after the 1952 Olympics, although the system was extensively used in America and on the Continent before that time. True, there were British athletes who saw the benefit of weight training and teachers like W. A. Pullum had used it with their pupils with success, but the majority of athletes and their trainers were a bit suspicious of its effects. Today, most top athletes, whatever their activity, use weight training to supplement their other methods.

General Principles

Train only twice a week, alternating your weight training nights with your athletic training nights. Use light weights and do three sets of a set number of repetitions, usually eight or ten, not training to the point of resistance as you did when body building. For squats, presses, upright rowing, bent over rowing and so on, a weight of 40 to 50lb will be sufficient; for dumb-bell exercises, 10 to 15lb. Do exercises that cover the full range of muscles and add one or two extra for the muscle groups you particularly use in your activity. Always warm up first with free-standing exercises; always relax at the end.

Sprinting

Sprinters need good leg development, the ability to make a fast get-away, and good lungs.

To warm up **Exercises 52 to 60.**

For general development:

Exercise 21 Press behind Neck with Barbell. 3 sets of 10.

Exercise 3 Bench Press. 3 sets of 10.

Exercise 43 Sit-ups with Weight. 3 sets of 10 with 10lb weight.

Exercise 5 Straight Arm Pullovers. 3 sets of 10.

Exercise 25 Squats with Barbell. 3 sets of 10.

For sprinting:

Exercise 27 Straddle Lift. 3 sets of 10. This will strengthen your legs.

Exercise 30 Iron Boots Leg Raise Sideways. 3 sets of 10 with boots only.

Exercise 33 Iron Boots Knee Raise. 3 sets of 10 with boots only.

OR:

Exercise 26 Squats with Barbell at Clean. 3 sets of 10.

Exercise 31 Iron Boots Leg Raise Backwards. 3 sets of 10 with boots only.

Exercise 34 Iron Boots Thigh Extension. 3 sets of 10 with boots only. (Note that with the last six exercises you use either one group or the other. Vary your practice by doing the first three in one session and the second three in the next.)

For a quick start in the sprint:

Exercise 26(a) Jumping Squats. 3 sets of 10 with a light weight to begin with, but finding out what weight you can manage as you progress.

Exercise 38 Heels Raise using Calf Machine. 3 sets of 10. If you do not have a calf machine, do 3 sets of **Exercise 28** Heels Raise with Barbell, instead.

To relax **Exercises 59 and 60.**

You may ask where the lung development and breathing comes into this work-out. The answer is mainly in the squats, which are powerful exercises for developing chest and lungs.

Middle and Long Distance Running
For this type of running you need good leg muscles and breathing, but you also need stamina to stay the course. The following programme worked at each training session should help.
To warm up **Exercises 52 to 60**.
For the legs:
Exercise 25 Squats with Barbell. 3 sets of 10.
Exercise 25(a) Jumping Squats. 3 sets of 10.
Exercise 28 Heels Raise with Barbell. 3 sets of 10, or, if you have a calf machine, 3 sets of **Exercise 38** Heels Raise using Calf Machine, instead.
Exercise 40 Hack Lift. 3 sets of 10.
For breathing and stamina:
Exercise 1 Bent Over Rowing. 3 sets of 10.
Exercise 5 Straight Arm Pullovers. 3 sets of 10.
Exercise 3 Bench Press. 3 sets of 10.
Exercise 7 Alternate Dumb-bell Presses. 3 sets of 10.
For the abdominal muscles:
Exercise 43: Sit-ups with Weight. 3 sets of 10 with 10lb weight.
Exercise 36 Legs Raise with Iron Boots from a Prone Position. 3 sets of 10 with boots only.
To relax **Exercises 59 and 60**.

Hurdling
Hurdlers need the same attributes as sprinters and jumpers, that is speed, a quick getaway, spring and co-ordination.
To warm up **Exercises 52 to 60**.
For the legs:
Exercise 25(a) Jumping Squats. 3 sets of 10.
Exercise 25 Squats with Barbell. 3 sets of 10.
Exercise 38 Heels Raise using Calf Machine. 3 sets of 10. If you do not have a calf machine, do 3 sets of **Exercise 28** Heels Raise with Barbell, instead.

For general development:
Exercise 7 Alternate Dumb-bell Presses. 3 sets of 10.
Exercise 2 Upright Rowing. 3 sets of 10.
Exercise 5 Straight Arm Pullovers. 3 sets of 10.
Exercise 46 Side Bends with Dumb-bells. 3 sets of 10.
Exercise 47 Trunk Turning with Dumb-bells. 3 sets of 10.
Exercise 43 Sit-ups with Weight. 3 sets of 10 with 10lb.
Exercise 36 Legs Raise from a Prone Position. 3 sets of 10 without iron boots.
To relax **Exercises 59 and 60**.

High Jump
Jumpers need strong leg muscles, agility and supple hips.
To warm up **Exercises 52 to 60**.
For the legs, EITHER:
Exercise 25 Squats with Barbell. 3 sets of 10.
Exercise 38 Heels Raise using Calf Machine. 3 sets of 10.
If you do not have a calf machine, 3 sets of 10 of **Exercise 28** Heels Raise with Barbell.
Exercise 30 Iron Boots Leg Raise Sideways. 3 sets of 8.
OR, on alternate practice nights:
Exercise 25(a) Jumping Squats. 3 sets of 10.
Exercise 31 Iron Boots Leg Raise Backwards. 3 sets of 10.
Exercise 32 Iron Boots Swing. 3 sets of 10.
Then, for general strength and suppleness:
Exercise 49 Trunk Turning with Bar across Shoulders. 3 sets of 10 each way with bar only.
Exercise 46 Side Bends with Dumb-bells. 3 sets of 10 each side.
Exercise 2 Upright Rowing. 3 sets of 10.
Exercise 7 Alternate Dumb-bell Presses. 3 sets of 10 each hand.
Finally, for the legs again:
Exercise 29 Seated Heels Raise with Barbell. 3 sets of 8.
To relax **Exercises 59 and 60**.

Long Jump

Long jumpers need speed for the run-up, leg strength and strong abdominals.

To warm up **Exercises 52 to 60.**

For general development:

Exercise 15 Press with Barbell. 3 sets of 10.

Exercise 16 Curls with Barbell. 3 sets of 10.

Exercise 5 Straight Arm Pullovers. 3 sets of 10.

For leg strength and take off, choose four or five of the following eleven exercises, varying your choice on different training nights, so that you work them all into your programme.

Exercise 25 Squats with Barbell. 3 sets of 10.

Exercise 25(a) Jumping Squats. 3 sets of 10.

Exercise 25(b) Half Squats. 3 sets of 10.

Exercise 38 Heels Raise using Calf Machine. 3 sets of 10. If you do not have a calf machine, do 3 sets of **Exercise 28** Heels Raise with Barbell, instead.

Exercise 29 Seated Heels Raise with Barbell. 3 sets of 10.

Exercise 27 Straddle Lift. 3 sets of 8.

Exercise 30 Iron Boots Leg Raise Sideways. 3 sets of 10.

Exercise 33 Iron Boots Knee Raise. 3 sets of 10.

Exercise 31 Iron Boots Leg Raise Backwards. 3 sets of 10.

Exercise 34 Iron Boots Thigh Extension. 3 sets of 8.

Exercise 26 Squats with Barbell at Clean. 3 sets of 10.

For the abdominals:

Exercise 43 Sit-ups with Weight. 3 sets of 10 with as much weight as you can manage.

Exercise 36 Legs Raise with Iron Boots from a Prone Position. 3 sets of 10.

To relax **Exercises 59 and 60.**

Pole Vault

Pole vaulters need strong arms, shoulders and abdominals.

To warm up **Exercises 52 to 60.**

If you have access to a pulley and weights, do:

Exercise 22 Back Lying Curl on Bench with Pulley and Weights. 3 sets of 10.

Exercise 12 Pull to Back of Neck using Pulley and Weights. 3 sets of 10.

Exercise 13 Pull to Chest on Incline Bench. 3 sets of 10.

If you do not have a pulley and weights, replace these three exercises with:

Exercise 16 Curls with Barbell. 3 sets of 10.

Exercise 21 Press behind Neck with Barbell. 3 sets of 10.

Exercise 6 Bent Arm Pullovers. 3 sets of 8.

Then go on to:

Exercise 5 Straight Arm Pullovers. 3 sets of 10.

Exercise 46 Side Bends with Dumb-bells. 3 sets of 10 each side.

Exercise 49 Trunk Turning with Bar across Shoulders. 3 sets of 10 each way.

Exercise 3 Bench Press. 3 sets of 10.

Exercise 18 Triceps Stretch Standing. 3 sets of 10.

Exercise 2 Upright Rowing. 3 sets of 10.

Exercise 43 Sit-ups with Weight. 3 sets of 10.

Exercise 36 Legs Raise with Iron Boots from a Prone Position. 3 sets of 8.

To relax **Exercises 59 to 60.**

Javelin

Javelin throwers need strong shoulders.

To warm up **Exercises 52 to 60.**

Exercise 5 Straight Arm Pullovers. 3 sets of 10.

Exercise 6 Bent Arm Pullovers. 3 sets of 8.

Exercise 3 Bench Press. 3 sets of 10.

Exercise 2 Upright Rowing. 3 sets of 10.

Exercise 7 Alternate Dumb-bell Presses. 3 sets of 10 each hand.

Exercise 9 Forward and Upward Swing with Dumb-bells. 3 sets each hand of 10 each.

Exercise 24 Dumb-bell Raises. 3 sets of 10 each hand.

Exercise 8 Lateral Raises. 3 sets of 10.

Exercise 18 Triceps Stretch Standing. 3 sets of 8.

Exercise 19 Triceps Stretch Seated. 3 sets of 8.

Exercise 25 Squats with Barbell. 3 sets of 10.
To relax **Exercises 59 and 60.**

Shot Put
Heavy men are best at this event; the fingers especially need strengthening.
To warm up **Exercises 52 to 60.**
Exercise 16 Curls with Barbell. 3 sets of 10.
Exercise 3 Bench Press. 3 sets of 10.
Exercise 25 Squats with Barbell. 3 sets of 10.
Exercise 21 Press behind Neck with Barbell. 3 sets of 10.
Exercise 46 Side Bends with Dumb-bells. 3 sets of 10.
Exercise 36 Legs Raise with Iron Boots from a Prone Position. 3 sets of 10.
Exercise 27 Straddle Lift. 3 sets with as much weight as you can manage.
Exercise 23 Wrist Roller Exercise. Roll up 3 times.
Exercise 17 Reverse Curls with Barbell. 3 sets with bar only of 8 per set.
Exercise 7 Alternate Dumb-bell Presses. 3 sets of 10.
To relax **Exercises 59 and 60.**

Discus
Discus throwers use the same muscles as javelin throwers but also especially need to develop the oblique abdominals.
To warm up **Exercises 52 to 60.**
Exercise 27 Straddle Lift. 3 sets of 8 with heaviest weight you can manage.
Exercise 46 Side Bends with Dumb-bells. 3 sets of 10 each side.

Exercise 49 Trunk Turning with Bar across Shoulders. 3 sets of 10 each way with a light weight on the bar, say 20lb.
Exercise 25 Squats with Barbell. 3 sets of 10.
Exercise 3 Bench Press. 3 sets of 10.
Exercise 16 Curls with Barbell. 3 sets of 10.
Exercise 2 Upright Rowing. 3 sets of 10.
Then do any three of the following six exercises, alternating them on different nights:
Exercise 4 Crucifix with Dumb-bells. 3 sets of 10.
Exercise 5 Straight Arm Pullovers. 3 sets of 10.
Exercise 6 Bent Arm Pullovers. 3 sets of 8.
Exercise 8 Lateral Raises. 3 sets of 10.
Exercise 7 Alternate Dumb-bell Presses. 3 sets of 10 each hand.
Exercise 24 Dumb-bell Raises. 3 sets of 10.
Finish with **Exercise 14** Clean with Barbell. 3 sets of 8.
To relax **Exercises 59 and 60.**

Some athletes, once they are experienced with this type of training, take to using heavy weights, but usually then they reduce the number of exercises to just two or three per evening, to develop a particular muscle that is needed. If, after you have trained for some time on the courses suggested in this chapter, you wish to follow other athletes in your particular event, study what the top men recommend and see if it suits you.

13 Weight Training for Other Sports

As with athletics, if you are using weight training to help with a sport, train only twice a week, alternating your weight training nights with your normal training nights. Use light weights, in some sports very light, as indicated; normally 40 to 50lb will be sufficient for the lifting exercises such as squats, bent over rowing, presses, etc, and 10lb should be ample on the dumb-bells. For most exercises work three sets of ten, not to the point of resistance as when body building.

Badminton
Players need speed and strong wrists.
To warm up **Exercises 52 to 60.**
Exercise 7 Alternate Dumb-bell Presses. 3 sets of 10 each hand.
Exercise 20 Single Arm Dumb-bell Curls. 3 sets of 10 each hand.
Exercise 25(a) Jumping Squats. 3 sets of 8.
Exercise 5 Straight Arm Pullovers. 3 sets of 8.
Exercise 46 Side Bends with Dumb-bells. 3 sets of 10 each side.
Exercise 36 Legs Raise with Iron Boots from a Prone Position. 3 sets of 10.
Exercise 23 Wrist Roller Exercise, 3 roll ups.
Exercise 17 Reverse Curls with Barbell. Use bar only. 3 sets of 10.
Exercise 8 Lateral Raises. 3 sets of 10.
Exercise 9 Forward and Upward Swing with Dumb-bells. 3 sets of 10.
To relax **Exercises 59 and 60.**

Boxing
Boxers need general all-round strength and fitness, good abdominals so that they can take punches in that region, strong shoulders and neck muscles, and fast footwork. They will therefore need all-round training, but must avoid using heavy weights to build up, as usually they are trying to keep their weight down.
To warm up **Exercises 52 to 60.**
Exercise 25(a) Jumping Squats. 3 sets of 20 instead of 10, but using only about 30lb in weight.
Exercise 24 Dumb-bell Raises. 3 sets of 10 with 5lb dumb-bells.
Exercise 17 Reverse Curls with Barbell. 3 sets of 10 with bar only.
Exercise 5 Straight Arm Pullovers. 3 sets of 8 with 10lb.
Exercise 7 Alternate Dumb-bell Presses. 3 sets of 10 with 5lb dumb-bells.
Exercise 2 Upright Rowing. 3 sets of 10 with 40lb.
Exercise 28 Heels Raise with Barbell. 3 sets of 10 with 30lb.
Exercise 35 Knees Raise with Iron Boots from a Prone Position. 3 sets of 10 with boots only.
Exercise 45 Legs Raise on Bench with Iron Boots. 3 sets of 10 with boots only.
Exercise 51 Side Bends with Dumb bell over Head. 3 sets of 10 each side with 10lb dumb-bell.
Then, try punching with a 5lb dumb-bell in each hand. 2 minute session.
To relax **Exercises 59 and 60.**

Cricket
Cricketers need strong abdominals, shoulders, arms and leg muscles.
To warm up **Exercises 52 to 60.**
Exercise 25 Squats with Barbell. 3 sets of 10.

Exercise 21 Press behind Neck with Barbell. 3 sets of 10.

Exercise 5 Straight Arm Pullovers. 3 sets of 10.

Exercise 14 Clean with Barbell. 3 sets of 10.

Exercise 27 Straddle Lift. 3 sets of 10 with as much weight as you can manage.

Exercise 24 Dumb-bell Raises. 3 sets of 10.

Exercise 8 Lateral Raises. 3 sets of 10.

Exercise 23 Wrist Roller Exercise. Roll up 3 times.

Exercise 45 Legs Raise on Bench with Iron Boots. 3 sets of 10, boots only.

Exercise 50 Sit-ups on Incline Bench with Weight. 3 sets of 10 with 10lb.

To relax **Exercises 59 and 60.**

Cycling

Cyclists need strong leg muscles, of course, and good chest development.

To warm up **Exercises 52 to 60.**

Exercise 25 Squats with Barbell. 3 sets of 10.

Exercise 3 Bench Press. 3 sets of 10.

Exercise 27 Straddle Lift. 3 sets of 10 with as much weight as you can manage.

Exercise 37 Leg Presses with Leg-pressing Machine. If you can get hold of such apparatus, 3 sets of 10 (if not do an extra set each of the three iron boot exercises below).

Exercise 1 Bent Over Rowing. 3 sets of 10.

Exercise 29 Seated Heels Raise with Barbell. 3 sets of 10.

Exercise 31 Iron Boots Leg Raise Backwards. 3 sets of 10 with boots only.

Exercise 32 Iron Boots Swing. 3 sets of 10 each leg, boots only.

Exercise 33 Iron Boots Knee Raise. 3 sets of 10, boots only.

To relax **Exercises 59 and 60.**

Fencing

Fencers need good thigh and calf muscles, also strong wrists and forearms.

To warm up **Exercises 52 to 60.**

Exercise 38 Heels Raise using Calf Machine. 3 sets of 10 or, if you do not have a calf machine, 3 sets of **Exercise 28** Heels Raise with Barbell.

Exercise 17 Reverse Curls with Barbell. 3 sets of 10.

Exercise 7 Alternate Dumb-bell Presses. 3 sets of 10.

Exercise 5 Straight Arm Pullovers. 3 sets of 10.

Exercise 24 Dumb-bell Raises. 3 sets of 10.

Exercise 23 Wrist Roller Exercise. 3 roll ups.

Exercise 25 Squats with Barbell. 3 sets of 10.

Exercise 2 Upright Rowing. 3 sets of 10.

Exercise 34 Iron Boots Thigh Extension. 3 sets of 10.

To relax **Exercises 59 and 60.**

Football

Footballers need a lot of leg exercises, the ability to run fast, and general all-round fitness.

To warm up **Exercises 52 to 60.**

Exercise 25(a) Jumping Squats. 3 sets of 10. (These will help with heading the ball.)

Exercise 38 Heels Raise using Calf Machine. 3 sets of 10 or, if you do not have a calf machine, 3 sets of **Exercise 28** Heels Raise with Barbell, instead.

Exercise 39 Step Up onto Bench with Weight on Shoulders. 3 sets of 10.

Exercise 34 Iron Boots Thigh Extension. 3 sets of 10. (This is particularly recommended by some authorities to footballers.)

Exercise 32 Iron Boots Swing. 3 sets of 10.

Exercise 51 Side Bends with Dumb-bell over Head. 3 sets of 10 each side.

Exercise 45 Legs Raise on Bench with Iron Boots. 3 sets of 10 with boots only.

Exercise 14 Clean with Barbell. 3 sets of 10.

Exercise 44 Legs Raise with Iron Boots using a Beam. 3 sets of 10 with boots only. If you do not have a beam, do **Exercise 33** Iron Boots Knee Raise, instead. 3 sets.

Exercise 15 Press with Barbell. 3 sets of 10.

To relax **Exercises 59 and 60.**

Rowing
Rowers need strong arms and shoulders, good abdominals and thigh muscles, and strong back muscles.
To warm up **Exercises 52 to 60.**
Exercise 20 Single Arm Dumb-bell Curls. 3 sets of 10.
Exercise 21 Press behind Neck with Barbell. 3 sets of 10.
Exercise 25(b) Half Squats. 3 sets of 10.
Exercise 43 Sit-ups with Weight. 3 sets of 10 with 10lb.
Exercise 45 Legs Raise on Bench with Iron Boots. 3 sets of 10 with boots only.
Exercise 34 Iron Boots Thigh Extension. 3 sets of 10 with boots only.
Exercise 27 Straddle Lift. 3 sets of 10 with as much weight as you can manage.
Exercise 40 Hack Lift. 3 sets of 10 with as much weight as you can manage.
Exercise 37 Leg Presses with Leg-pressing Machine. 3 sets of 10. If you do not have a leg pressing machine, do 3 sets of **Exercise 33** Iron Boots Knee Raise, instead.
Exercise 10 Single Hand Rowing. 3 sets of 10.
To relax **Exercises 59 and 60.**

Rugby
Rugby players need good arm and shoulder development, and are generally bigger and more muscular all round than footballers.
To warm up **Exercises 52 to 60.**
Exercise 16 Curls with Barbell. 3 sets of 10.
Exercise 3 Bench Press. 3 sets of 10.
Exercise 25(b) Half Squats. 3 sets of 10.
Exercise 1 Bent Over Rowing. 3 sets of 10.
Exercise 36 Legs Raise with Iron Boots from a Prone Position. 3 sets of 10.
Exercise 43 Sit-ups with Weight. 3 sets of 10 with 10lb.
Exercise 49 Trunk Turning with Bar across Shoulders. 3 sets of 10 with 20lb on bar.
Exercise 46 Side Bends with Dumb-bells. 3 sets of 10 each side.

Exercise 12 Pull to Back of Neck using Pulley and Weights. 3 sets of 10. If you do not have a pulley, do 3 sets of **Exercise 21** Press behind Neck with Barbell, instead.
Exercise 2 Upright Rowing. 3 sets of 10.
To relax **Exercises 59 and 60.**

Swimming
Swimmers need good lungs, stamina and strength, and extra power in the arms would be useful. A general course with some extra arm work is therefore indicated.
To warm up **Exercises 52 to 60.**
Exercise 25 Squats with Barbell. 3 sets of 10.
Exercise 16 Curls with Barbell. 3 sets of 10.
Exercise 15 Press with Barbell. 3 sets of 10.
Exercise 1 Bent Over Rowing. 3 sets of 10.
Exercise 5 Straight Arm Pullovers. 3 sets of 10.
Exercise 6 Bent Arm Pullovers. 3 sets of 10.
Exercise 12 Pull to Back of Neck using Pulley and Weights. 3 sets of 10. If you do not have pulley and weights, do 3 sets of **Exercise 21** Press behind Neck with Barbell, instead.
Exercise 32 Iron Boots Swing. 3 sets of 10 each leg.
Exercise 33 Iron Boots Knee Raise. 3 sets of 10 with boots only.
Exercise 2 Upright Rowing. 3 sets of 10.
To relax **Exercises 59 and 60.**

Tennis
Tennis players need speed and good arm and shoulder muscles, so very light weights are indicated.
To warm up **Exercises 52 to 60.**
Exercise 25(a) Jumping Squats. 3 sets of 10.
Exercise 16 Curls with Barbell. 3 sets of 10.
Exercise 17 Reverse Curls with Barbell. 3 sets of 10 with bar only.
Exercise 8 Lateral Raises. 3 sets of 10 with 5lb dumb-bells.

Exercise 7 Alternate Dumb-bell Presses. 3 sets of 10 with 5lb dumb-bells.

Exercise 46 Side Bends with Dumb-bells. 3 sets of 10 each side with 5lb dumb-bells.

Exercise 47 Trunk Turning with Dumb-bells. 3 sets of 10 each way with 5lb dumb-bells.

Exercise 5 Straight Arm Pullovers. 3 sets of 10.

Exercise 23 Wrist Roller Exercise. 3 roll ups.

To relax **Exercises 59 and 60**.

Wrestling

Wrestlers need all-round strength and often enter the profession from other sports such as body building, boxing or rugby, or start in the amateur ranks. Good abdominals, legs and shoulder muscles are needed, and heavier weights could be used for strength. Some Indian wrestlers are said to train with just two free-standing exercises, the Deep Knees Bend **Exercise 52** and the Cat Stretch. This consists of taking the weight on the palms of the hands and on the toes, with the chest upright and the back concave. From this position the back is arched upwards by lowering the head and raising the buttocks, so that the back becomes convex. You then return to the original position. They do an enormous number, something like 3,000 per day. The following course should help amateur and would-be wrestlers. Sets to be of ten repetitions but if you cannot manage this number, work up to it and increase the weight you are using when you go beyond twelve repetitions.

To warm up **Exercises 52 to 60**.

Exercise 25 Squats with Barbell. 3 sets with 60lb if you can manage.

Exercise 16 Curls with Barbell. 3 sets with 60lb.

Exercise 15 Press with Barbell. 3 sets with 60lb.

Exercise 4 Crucifix with Dumb-bells. 3 sets with 10lb.

Exercise 3 Bench Press. 3 sets with 60lb.

Exercise 1 Bent Over Rowing. 3 sets with 60lb.

Exercise 27 Straddle Lift. 3 sets with as much weight as you can manage.

Exercise 40 Hack Lift. 3 sets with as much weight as you can manage.

Exercise 45 Legs Raise on Bench with Iron Boots. 3 sets with boots only.

Exercise 50 Sit-ups on Incline Bench with Weight. 3 sets with 15lb.

To relax **Exercises 59 and 60**.

You will notice that many exercises are common to all the courses. The difference in training between individual sports is a slight emphasis on the particular muscles needed. It is essential to use specific exercises within the context of general development, otherwise your development will be disproportionate, especially if you are only just beginning to use weights. It is true that advanced sportsmen with considerable experience of physical training may use fewer exercises and may concentrate on one or two muscle groups only, but this is bad for a beginner and not altogether wise at any stage.

14 Weight Training for Women

For a long time weight training was considered a man's world, but in recent years women have become more and more involved. They can train for all-round fitness, for suppleness and poise, to correct defects such as slack stomach muscles or sagging bust, to reduce weight, or to aid other sports.

Most of the exercises specified for men can also be done by women with the same effect but, in general, women use lower poundages, and they should be wary of the overhead lifts such as the Press with Barbell **Exercise 15** until they have first done some strengthening exercises for the trunk and lower back. It may be inadvisable to train during the monthly periods. Women should use their discretion. If a woman followed the body building course in Chapter 10, albeit with lighter weights and perhaps fewer repetitions, she would develop her physique in the same way as a man would, but most women do not want bulging muscles or to become an Amazon. They are content with fitness. Certainly a much less strenuous course will give them robust health, as it will not only improve their outward physique but will also strengthen all their internal organs as well.

The advice given in Chapter 2 on how and when to train is as applicable to women as to men, of course. They should wear a brassière with broad shoulder straps that will not cut into them and pants, and can wear a track suit, or trousers and a T-shirt, if this is comfortable. They should pay particular attention to the warming-up exercises, as some women maintain health with these and nothing else, but since this book is about weight training we shall of course consider the use of weights.

For All-round Fitness
Train three nights a week, with a night's rest in between. The most suitable time would be the evening, at least an hour after the last meal.
To warm up **Exercises 52 to 60.**
Exercise 24 Dumb-bell Raises. 3 sets with 5lb dumb-bells. 10 in each set.
Exercise 25 Squats with Barbell. 3 sets of 10 with about 30lb. (Note that the bar itself will weigh about 10lb, so take this into account.) Women must be particularly sure in this exercise that they are wearing shoes with heels, though not high heels of course, and that they keep the back upright.
Exercise 5 Straight Arm Pullovers. 3 sets of 10 with 5lb weight.
Exercise 41 Good Morning Exercise with Barbell. Initially do 2 sets with 30lb, 8 in each set, and work up to 3 sets of 10. This will greatly strengthen the back, preparatory to any overhead lifts.
Exercise 3 Bench Press. 3 sets of 10 with 30lb.
Exercise 46 Side Bends with Dumb-bells. 2 sets of 10 each side, working up to 3 sets of 10 with 5lb dumb-bells.
Exercise 36 Legs Raise from a Prone Position, but without the iron boots. Ordinary shoes will be heavy enough. 2 sets of 10 working up to 3 sets of 10, and only coming to iron boots after at least a year's training.
Exercise 43 Sit-ups, but without the weight to begin with. 3 sets of 8 working up to 3 sets of 10 then, after a year or so,

using a 5lb weight and later a 10lb weight.

Exercise 28 Heels Raise with Barbell, using the bar only. 2 sets of 8 working up to 3 sets of 10.

To relax **Exercises 59 and 60.**

After following this course for six months, during which time the back will be strengthened by the squats and the Good Morning exercise, you can also include **Exercise 8** Lateral Raises with 5lb dumb-bells. 2 sets of 8 working up to 3 sets of 10.

Followed regularly, this course will keep you fit, promote a strong healthy body, and make you feel on top of the world.

For Suppleness and Poise
Use very low poundages on this course; these will produce stamina rather than strength and will keep you graceful and agile.

To warm up **Exercises 52 to 60.**

Exercise 45 Legs Raise on Bench, but without using iron boots. 2 sets of 8 working up to 3 sets of 10.

Exercise 9 Forward and Upward Swing with Dumb-bells. 2 sets of 8 working up to 3 sets of 10. Use 5lb dumb-bells.

Exercise 46 Side Bends with Dumb-bells. 2 sets of 8 working up to 3 sets of 10 with 5lb dumb-bells.

Exercise 30 Leg Raise Sideways, but without the iron boots. 2 sets of 8 working up to 3 sets of 10.

Exercise 25 Squats with Barbell, but with bar only. 2 sets of 8 working up to 3 sets of 10.

Exercise 43 Sit-ups, but without weight for the first six months. 2 sets of 8 working up to 3 sets of 10 and dropping back to 2 sets of 8 when you start using a weight.

Exercise 5 Straight Arm Pullovers. 2 sets of 8 working up to 3 sets of 10 with 5lb.

To relax **Exercises 59 and 60.**

Only after following this for six months should you add the following:

Exercise 21 Press behind Neck with Barbell, with the bar only for a further six months before adding 20lb.

For Slack Stomach Muscles
If sagging of the stomach muscles is your problem, you need the abdominal exercises, and can do three or four each training period, or simply concentrate on this area with the free-standing warming-up exercises as the only addition. The following programme should help.

To warm up **Exercises 52 to 60.**

Exercise 36 Legs Raise with Iron Boots from a Prone Position. Start with 1 set of 10 without boots. Work up over a period of weeks to 3 sets of 10 without boots. Then drop back to 1 set of 8 with boots only, and work up over a period of weeks to 3 sets of 10 with boots only. Never do more than you can accomplish without strain and do not force yourself to the point of resistance as body builders do.

Exercise 43 Sit-ups with Weight. Do 1 set of 10 without weight and work up to 3 sets of 10 with weight of 10lb in the same way as for the last exercise. Again, do not force yourself to the point of resistance. You are not trying to build up your muscles, but rather to tone them up so that they will fulfil their function.

Exercise 33 Iron Boots Knee Raise. Do 1 set of 10 without boots and work up to 3 sets of 10 without. Then drop back to 1 set of 8 with boots only and work up to 3 sets of 10 with boots. Do not force yourself.

Exercise 45 Legs Raise on Bench with Iron Boots. 1 set of 10 without boots, working up in the same progression as before to 3 sets of 10 with boots.

To relax **Exercises 59 and 60.**

This work-out should take you about fifteen to twenty minutes and can be done three times a week, on alternate nights.

For the Bust
To warm up **Exercises 52 to 60.**

86

Exercise 4 Crucifix with Dumb-bells. Do 1 set of 10 with 5lb dumb-bells, working up to 3 sets of 10 over a period of two to three months.
Exercise 5 Straight Arm Pullovers. 1 set of 10 with 5lb, working up to 3 sets of 10 with 10lb dumb-bell over three months.
Exercise 2 Upright Rowing. 1 set of 10 with bar only, working up to 3 sets of 10 with 30lb.
Exercise 3 Bench Press. 1 set of 10 with 20lb, working up to 3 sets of 10 with 30lb.
Exercise 7 Alternate Dumb-bell Presses. 1 set of 10 each hand with 5lb dumb-bells, working up to 3 sets of 10.
To relax **Exercises 59 and 60.**

Again, do not force yourself. Practise three times a week on alternate nights.

For the Hips
To warm up **Exercises 52 to 60.**
Exercise 46 Side Bends with Dumb-bells. 1 set of 10 each side with 5lb dumb-bells, working up to 3 sets of 20 each side with 10lb dumb-bells.
Exercise 47 Trunk Turning with Dumb-bells. 1 set of 10 each side with 5lb dumb-bells, working up to 3 sets of 20 each side, still with 5lb dumb-bells.
To relax **Exercises 59 and 60.**

Practise three times a week, on alternate nights.

For Slimming
To slim you have to use very low poundages with high repetitions and avoid at all costs working to the point of resistance, as this would build you up. A one-set system is therefore indicated, using exercises that cover all the muscle groups in turn.
To warm up **Exercises 52 to 60.**
Exercise 25 Squats with bar only. 20 repetitions working up to 30.
Exercise 7 Alternate Dumb-bell Presses. 2½lb dumb-bells, and 20 each hand, working up to 30, in 1 set only.
Exercise 5 Straight Arm Pullovers. 1 set of 20 with 5lb, working up to 1 set of 30.

Exercise 2 Upright Rowing, with bar only. 1 set of 20 working up to 30.
Exercise 4 Crucifix with Dumb-bells, using 2½lb dumb-bells. 1 set of 20 working up to 1 set of 30.
Exercise 47 Trunk Turning with Dumb-bells. 1 set of 20 each side working up to 1 set of 30, using 5lb dumb-bells.
Exercise 46 Side Bends with Dumb-bells. 1 set of 20 each side working up to 1 set of 30, using 5lb dumb-bells.
Exercise 43 Sit-ups, but without weight. 1 set of 10, working up as you are able to 1 set of 40, but no weight.
Exercise 45 Legs Raise on Bench, but without iron boots. 1 set of 10 working up to 1 set of 40.
To relax **Exercises 59 and 60.**

Try to do the exercises quickly and rhythmically in this course. Do not strain and do not attempt more than you can easily manage. Follow the course three times a week, with a night's rest in between. It should take you about twenty minutes a night.

You will succeed in slimming only if you combine the exercises with a suitable diet. Exercises alone will not help you slim; they simply tone up the body so that the digestive and excretory processes function better together with all the body's systems. It has been estimated that to lose 1lb in body weight, you would have to do exercise equivalent to walking sixty miles. After such an amount of exercise, you would probably be so hungry that you would eat more and so immediately put the pound back on again.

Finally, women may use exercises to help with other sports. In this case they may follow the plans outlined in Chapters 12 and 13, according to their chosen activity, but they should use considerably lower poundages than men. Dumb-bells of 2½ to 5lb are indicated and the bar alone can be used for some exercises, but never with more than 30lb, counting the weight of the bar. It might also be better for women to begin with one set of each exercise and work up to two or three sets as suggested in the various courses but this depends on the individual's strength and fitness.

Of course, if development of a particular muscle is desired, three sets of the appropriate exercise to the point of resistance are needed, but bear in mind that this will make the muscle bigger and it may be unsightly or out of proportion to your physique as a whole. You must decide what you want in this case and carefully work out a training programme which will suit your own individual requirements.

15 Weight Lifting and Power Lifting

There are two separate competitive sports, weight lifting and power lifting. Weight lifting is controlled by the International Weight Lifting Federation, which was founded in 1920, and the British Amateur Weightlifters Association is the member association responsible for the sport in this country. Power lifting is controlled in the same way by the International Power Lifting Federation, which was founded in 1972.

Weight training is an essential preparation for taking part in these sports and the beginner would do well to start with the training programme in Chapter 10. When he starts weight lifting or power lifting, however, he must join a club, as he will need helpers to take the very heavy weights off him in some of the lifts and expert coaching to make sure that he is performing the lifts correctly without risk of injury and in the form recognised for competitions by the national body. To attempt to learn from a book might lead to errors of style which would be very difficult afterwards to eradicate, and to practise on one's own might lead to accident.

For these reasons, no illustrations are given in this chapter, which is concerned solely with explaining the sports. If you go to a coach who is recognised by one of the international bodies, you will receive expert instruction and will be able to practise without serious risk. Given this supervision, it should be said that the accident rate is very low compared with other sports.

The International Weight Lifting Federation recognises two lifts, which must be taken in sequence:

1 The Two Hands Snatch

The rules of the snatch are that the bar should be placed horizontally in front of the lifter's legs. He grips it palms downwards and in a single movement pulls it from the ground to the full extent of both arms overhead. There are two styles of doing this:

(i) **The Squat Method** In this the lifter pulls the bar upwards and dips under it in a low squat.

(ii) **The Split or Fore and Aft Method** In this the lifter pulls the bar upwards and goes under it with a lunge, whereby one foot goes to the front and one to the rear.

Either is acceptable, but when the bar is overhead it must be held motionless in that position, the arms and legs extended on the same line, until the referee gives the signal to replace the bar. The turning of the wrists must not take place until the bar has passed the top of the lifter's head.

Apart from a general training course, exercises which would particularly help this movement are:

Exercise 41 Good Morning Exercise with Barbell.

Exercise 1 Bent Over Rowing.

Exercise 2 Upright Rowing, with a shoulder width grip.

Exercise 7 Alternate Dumb-bell Presses.

Exercise 23 Wrist Roller Exercise.

Exercise 25 Squats, with bar only.

Three other exercises are also helpful:

Lunging with Dumb-bells in Hands Take a dumb-bell in each hand, hands on hips, feet in line. Now step forward with the right foot a distance twice the width of your shoulders, at the same time punching with your right hand at an imaginary opponent's stomach, head and chest upright. Bring the right foot and hand back, and do the same thing with the left foot and hand. Continue alternating hands.

Chinning a Beam Hang from a beam by the arms, with either an over or under grip (as preferred), feet clear of the ground. Chinning consists of pulling yourself up to look over the beam by bending your arms, then lowering to the hanging position.

Throwing a Light Dumb-bell Hand to Hand Take a five pound dumb-bell in one hand, and simply toss it from hand to hand, catching it, as if it were a ball. It needs dexterity and develops wrist and forearms.

2 The Two Hands Clean and Jerk

The rules of this lift are that the bar must be placed horizontally in front of the lifter's legs. He grips it palms down and takes it in a single movement from the ground to the shoulders, while either splitting or squatting. The bar then rests on the clavicles or chest and the legs are returned to the same line, straight, for the performance of the jerk. When the bar passes the hips the wrists are turned as described in Exercise 14, Clean with Barbell. The jerk which takes the bar to the arms extended overhead position is invariably executed with splitting. The bar must be held in the final position motionless until the referee gives the signal to replace it.

Exercises which would help are:
Exercise 41 Good Morning Exercise with Barbell.

Exercise 27 Straddle Lift.
Exercise 24 Dumb-bell Raises.
Exercise 25 Squats with Barbell.
Exercise 25(a) Jumping Squats.
Exercise 14 Clean with Barbell.
Exercise 21 Press behind Neck with Barbell.
Exercise 15 Press with Barbell.

Additionally, shoulder shrugging with dumb-bells in hand, and gripping exercises, such as squeezing a tennis ball, would be useful.

The weights achieved in the Snatch and the Two Hands Clean and Jerk are added together in competition to give a combined total. As an example of what can be achieved, in the 1976 Olympics David Rigert made a Snatch of 374¾lb and a Clean and Jerk of 468¼lb in the Middle Heavyweight division. There are nine divisions and the combined lifts achieved in these at the 1976 Olympics are shown below.

Psychological factors are involved in competitive lifting and this is where a good coach will be able to help. He must know when his charge needs stimulating to greater effort and when he needs to take a break and relax. He must understand the motivation of the lifter. Does he want to prove himself? Is he doing it for his club or his country? Almost invariably the lifter will be tense before a major competition. The coach will understand whether it is best to let him alone or to try to take his mind off the forthcoming event for a while.

Power lifters generally attempt one of three types of lift, though there are sometimes local competitions for other

Division	Body weight		Combined lift	
Flyweight	114½lb	52kg	535lb	242.68kg
Bantamweight	123½lb	56kg	579lb	262.63kg
Featherweight	132½lb	60kg	628lb	284.86kg
Lightweight	149lb	67.5kg	678lb	307.54kg
Middleweight	165½lb	75kg	738½lb	334.98kg
Light Heavyweight	182lb	82.5kg	805lb	365.15kg
Middle Heavyweight	198½lb	90kg	843lb	382.38kg
Heavyweight	242½lb	110kg	882lb	400.08kg
Superheavyweight	over 242½lb	over 110kg	970lb	439.99kg

feats of strength. The major ones, however, are:

1 The Deep Knees Bend or Squat

This is a test of leg and hip strength. The lifter takes the bar from squat stands, feet under the bar, legs normal width apart, back flat and inclined slightly forwards before the grip is taken. The bar rests on the back of the neck above the shoulder blades and the trapezius muscle provides a cushion against the heavy weight.

The lifter steps back to clear the stands. The feet are now approximately hip width apart, the toes pointing slightly outwards. When the referee gives the signal the competitor does the deep knees bend, breathing in before going down and out as he comes up. He must finish in an upright position with the knees, hips and shoulders in line.

Exercises which would help are:
Exercise 41 Good Morning Exercise with Barbell.
Exercise 37 Leg Presses with Leg Pressing Machine.
Exercise 25 Squats with Barbell, varying them to 25(b) Half Squats and even 25(c) Quarter Squats.
Exercise 40 Hack Lift.

2 The Bench Press

For this, the head, neck and body must lie flat on a bench, and the lifter may either have his feet on the floor, or have them raised and resting on a second bench. Loaders hand the bar to the lifter, who takes the widest and most comfortable grip. He lowers it onto his chest. He then awaits the referee's signal. On the signal, he presses the bar to an arm's length position over the shoulders, breathing out as he does so and pressing his feet into the ground, or

down on the second bench.

Exercises that would help are:
Exercise 15 Press with Barbell.
Exercise 3 Bench Press.
Exercise 24 Dumb-bell Raises.
Exercise 8 Lateral Raises.
Exercise 16 Curls with Barbell.

3 The Dead Lift

To begin, the bar is horizontal in front of the lifter's feet. He grips it with both hands with an optional grip. He then has to lift it in one continuous movement until he is standing erect. At the completion of the lift, his knees must be locked and his shoulders thrown back. The referee's signal that he recognises the lift is given when the bar is held motionless in the final position. It is then lowered under control.

The lifter should breathe in before lifting and out as he lifts. If he reverses his grip it will prevent the bar turning. His feet should be normal distance apart and his hands a little wider than shoulder width.

Exercises that would help are:
Exercise 27 Straddle Lift.
Exercise 41 Good Morning Exercise with Barbell.
Exercise 40 Hack Lift.
Exercise 1 Bent Over Rowing.
Exercise 23 Wrist Roller Exercise.

It would be pointless to suggest the number of repetitions of these training exercises, as the lifter should be guided by his coach who will know his individual needs and capacities.

Competitions are held locally and nationally in these events, and weight lifting is included in the Olympic Games, so for those to whom competition appeals, this can be the goal of their weight training.

Index